**Sun Myung Moon:
A Korean evangelist
whose influence
in America spreads daily.
What lies behind him?**

THE PUPPET MASTER

J. ISAMU YAMAMOTO

An Inquiry into
Sun Myung Moon
and the
Unification Church

InterVarsity Press
Downers Grove
Illinois 60515

A booklet by J. Isamu Yamamoto
The Moon Doctrine (IVP, 25¢)

InterVarsity Press is the book publishing
division of Inter-Varsity Christian Fellowship,
a student movement active on campus
at hundreds of universities, colleges and
schools of nursing.
For information about local and regional
activities, write IVCF, 233 Langdon St.,
Madison, WI 53703.

Bible quotations are from the
Revised Standard Version of the Bible,
copyrighted 1946, 1952, © 1971, 1973 by the
Division of Christian Education of the
National Council of Churches of Christ,
and are used by permission.

Cover: Illustration by
Kurt Mitchell

ISBN 0-87784-740-1

Library of Congress Catalog
Card Number: 76-55622

Printed in the United States of America

to my father and mother

1

SUN MYUNG MOON

11

THE UNIFICATION CHURCH

111

THE DIVINE PRINCIPLE

IV

CHRIST JESUS

PREFACE

A WOMAN, ABOUT FORTY, SMALL, with a tired expression on her face and with tears in her eyes, approached me. I was at the University of Wisconsin in Milwaukee and had just finished giving a talk on the Rev. Sun Myung Moon and the Unification Church. Most of my listeners were college students, but some like this woman were parents of students.

I realized that she was motivated by something deeper than curiosity. So I quickly dispensed with the questions asked by others, while she patiently waited. Finally, when we were able to be alone, she proceeded to share her story.

About two years ago her son was a senior at Boston College. At the end of the term he was to graduate and marry a young woman to whom he had been engaged for a year. His dream was smashed, however, when she left him for another man.

Extremely despondent, he drifted for another month at college until he encountered some representatives of the Unification Church. Excited by their demonstration of love and joy, he quit college and joined their movement. Since then he has rejected everything and everybody outside of the movement.

He wrote to his mother a month after becoming a follower of Moon, but that was the last she has heard from him. The authorities have told her that they cannot help because he is an adult. She has hired a detective to locate him, but with no success. And so her question: "What can I do to get my son back?"

A couple of months later, I was speaking at George Washington University in Washington, D. C. before another crowd. While I again lectured on Rev. Moon and his church, I noticed a young woman sitting alone in the back of the room. What caught my attention was the expressions of criticism on her face during my talk. I was sure she was a member of the Unification Church.

After the lecture, she confirmed my suspicions. She commended me on my talk, what she thought was fairly objective. She had heard that I was speaking and had assumed that my presentation would be another tirade against Rev. Moon. She was happy that it was not. Her only objection was that I did not fully understand Moon's doctrine. She invited me to come to her church to receive a full explanation of each point which I had discussed.

As we talked, I became deeply impressed by her past experience with the Unification Church. She told me that she had been in the movement once before. Her parents in desperation had kidnapped her and had hired Ted Patrick to deprogram her. He succeeded. Everything Ted Patrick said about Moon's wealth and the lifestyle of the church was true. He had totally convinced her to leave the movement at the time.

A year later, however, she rejoined the Unification Church. Being outside of it, there was a big void in her life which nothing else could fill. She had found meaning within the church, and she could not be happy unless she returned, despite its failings.

Recently I received a telephone call from a distraught husband, whose wife had just joined the Unification Church. He explained that he and his wife had been happily married for eight months and that she had graduated from art school a month ago. She had been invited to a dinner by some people she had met selling flowers at her graduation. That evening she phoned her husband to ask if she could attend a weekend seminar at Booneville, California. He gave his permission, still not suspecting who they were.

After a week of silence, however, he became extremely anxious for her welfare. Then she called again. She told him that she had joined the movement of love and fraternity and that she was forsaking everything for it. Her idealism, he said, had finally found a cause.

He went to visit her only to realize that she was dead serious. She would not leave with him. When he returned a second time with her brother, neither was allowed to see her. He then tried to obtain legal custody of her through the courts. When law officials went to Booneville, they discovered that she was gone. Later, the Unification Church produced her along with a lawyer.

In court he and his wife decided to spend a weekend alone to discuss the matter. While the court, the church and relatives anxiously awaited the outcome, they emerged from their seclusion. The wife had decided to return to the church. The husband would honor her desires, but he still expressed hope that someday she would return to him.

These are not isolated cases. I am constantly deluged by letters and phone calls, and I am personally approached by people who are experiencing similar tragedies in their families. Nor are these cases uniquely associated with Rev. Moon and his church. Many spiritual groups are now actively seeking converts in our society and wreaking havoc in the lives of thousands of families.

Rev. Moon and the Unification Church may be widely known because of the current publicity, but they are by no means alone. By understanding how he and his Unification Church operate and what the appeal of his church is, however, perhaps we can understand why such groups succeed. Then we can respond with more than stories of friends and relatives disappearing into strange new movements.

This book is divided into four sections. The first section contains the biography of Rev. Moon and his rise to prominence religiously, economically and politically. The second deals with his movement, primarily focusing on the Unification Church—its background, its religious practices and, most importantly, the conversion and indoctrination of its adherents. The third section discusses both the doctrines of the *Divine Principle* and the inner teachings, all of which originated from Moon. Finally, the fourth section presents a Christian evaluation of the movement suggesting how the gospel of Christ can be shared with the followers of Moon, explaining how Moon's doctrines depart from the Scriptures, and evaluating the role of Moon and his church play in today's struggle between God and Satan.

I would like to thank my brothers and sisters in Christ whose friendships, prayers and support have sustained me in my ministry. I would also like to thank and acknowledge the Spiritual Counterfeits Project (P. O. Box 4309, Berkeley, CA 94704), which is engaged in presenting the love and truth of Christ wherever the occult and Eastern mysticism emerge in our society.

J. Isamu Yamamoto
San Jose, California
November 1976

1

"AND CALL NO MAN
YOUR FATHER ON EARTH,
FOR YOU HAVE ONE FATHER,
WHO IS IN HEAVEN.
NEITHER BE CALLED MASTERS,
FOR YOU HAVE
ONE MASTER, THE CHRIST."

(MATTHEW 23:9-10)

THE
MASTER

1

REVEREND MOON OF SOUTH KOREA has gained worldwide recognition in the seventies as a controversial religious leader. As founder and head of the Unification Church and its affiliate organizations, Moon is frequently attacked. The press calls him a charlatan who is after political and economic power, parent groups insist that he is a spiritual dictator who has psychologically enslaved many of the youth of our society, and Christians see him as a heretic who has perverted the gospel of Christ Jesus. Nevertheless, very little is known of the man himself, except for his present activities in the United States. Certainly Moon is without question the first evangelist from the Orient, purporting Christianity, to truly bring his church into the mainstream of American religion.

The Vision/   Sun Myung Moon, who is referred to by his followers as Father or Master, was born on January 6, 1920, in the village of Kwangju Sangsa Ri, within the Pyungan Bukedo province in northwestern Korea. He is the second son in a family of eight, having one brother and six sisters. His father was a farmer.

When Moon was ten years old, his family converted to Christianity and became members of the Presbyterian Church. It was at this time that Moon decided that he wanted to be a great scholar and attain several degrees in different fields. After attending village primary school, he went to high school in the southern city of Seoul, where he attended a Pentecostal Church.

At fifteen, however, Moon's view of the world changed. According to his followers, Moon experienced a revelation similar to that of Buddha's. He realized that all of mankind from generation to generation had suffered the same struggles and sins, and that, if he died with the world unchanged, future generations would suffer as well. He wanted to liberate everyone—past, present and future—from this suffering. From then on he decided to bear the responsibility for relieving the burden of suffering from the human race.

On Easter morning in 1936, Moon was deep in prayer on a Korean mountainside when he had a vision. He relates that Jesus appeared to him and told him that he was chosen to complete the mission Jesus had started 2,000 years ago. Yet he hesitated, he says, because he knew that he could never turn back if he promised to fulfill this mission before God and Jesus. Moon further relates that Jesus said that "he [Moon] was the only one who could do it, and asked him again and again."[1] Finally, Moon says that he accepted the task, knowing that there would be no one to replace him if he failed.

For the next nine years, Moon prepared himself for that mission. In Seoul he spent most of his time in prayer. He discovered that God was lonely and grieving for the sins of man. He says that, when he understood the tragic life of Jesus, he cried for days. During this time he fought fierce spiritual battles against those forces which were trying to turn him away from his mission. Moon once said, "If anyone knew what I passed through during those years, his heart would stop in shock and sorrow. No one is capable of bearing this story."[2]

The Early Years/   During World War II, Moon attended
Waseda University in Tokyo, where he studied electrical engineering. It is unclear whether he actually graduated. In 1945,
after the Japanese occupation of Korea terminated, he began to
make known his revelations. In about 1948, Moon was excom-
municated by the Korean Presbyterian Church, which has con-
tinually condemned his revelations and doctrines.

In 1944, Moon returned to northern Korea and established a
following of his own. Two years later he traveled to southern
Korea where he met Paik Moon Kim whose name means "100
Gold Letters." This man, six years Moon's senior, familiar with
the prophecy of a Korean messiah, considered himself a savior
and declared it publicly. In Paju, a town north of Seoul and
near the 38th parallel, Kim established a community called
Israel Soodo Won (Israel Monastery), where Moon spent six
months. There he learned what was to become the basis of his
own theology as set forth in the *Divine Principle.* He then returned to his followers in Pyongyang, and in 1946 he established
the Kang Hei Church, meaning "Broad Sea Church," and began
preaching.

It was during this period that he changed his birth name of
Yong Myung Moon to Sun Myung Moon. To many people
Yong means "dragon." *Myung* means "bright," and *Moon* is
a common surname, which means "letter," "character," or
"writing." The character for *Sun* signifies "propriety" or
"goodness." Since 1946, therefore, he has used a name which
means "Shining Proper Letter."

In North Korea at that time, the communist regime persecuted Christians. On August 11, 1946, the communist police
jailed Moon. He claims that he was tortured by beating and
with lack of food and sleep. In the booklet *The Heart of Our
Father* Moon's suffering for his faith is likened to the suffering
of Christ. After he had attracted a small group of disciples
in war-torn North Korea, "the police came and an innocent
man [Moon] received a terrible beating, pints of blood flowed
from an internal injury. He lost consciousness. His broken

body was thrown outside the Daedong Police Station onto the frozen ground. Other disciples carried it away for a Christian burial. The catacomb existence of the underground saint began."[3]

For the following fifteen months, however, Moon continued his preaching without much interference. Then in February of 1948 the communists arrested him a second time. He received a five-year sentence at hard labor. In May he was sent to a concentration camp at Hung Nam where he spent the next two and a half years. The Unification Church has released stories of Moon's experiences at this camp, describing the hell he had to go through and how he survived. They say that he not only had to overcome insurmountable odds just to remain alive but that his personality and behavior throughout the ordeal were such a beautiful testimony to his faith and courage that the other prisoners became touched by his presence and even became followers.

Whether he was imprisoned because of his anti-communist activities or because of the complaints of other Christians who were jealous of him, Moon suffered terribly according to his followers. Meanwhile, Moon's critics reject these stories and the reasons for his imprisonment as fabrications to glorify him. They claim that he was sent to prison because of adultery. They also point out that Moon's anti-communist campaign did not start until 1962.

Just as the facts are uncertain as to the cause and the circumstances of his imprisonment, so there are various reports concerning Moon's deliverance out of the hands of the communists. One account states that on October 14, 1950, the day before it was his turn to be shot (after realizing that they had to withdraw, the communists decided to shoot their prisoners), he escaped when a bombardment by the United Nations Forces caused his guards to flee. Another is that in the winter of 1950-1951 he was released from prison by the United Nations Forces at Hungnam.

In any case, Moon returned to South Korea as a refugee with

two or three disciples. Only one cousin of his survived to collaborate the details of Moon's early life. The rest of his family was either killed or lost behind the Bamboo Curtain after the Korean War.

The Founding of His Church/   Moon settled at Pusan where he became a harbor laborer between 1950 and 1954. Also, during this time, he began to teach the Principles, which were formulated by Moon and a man in Pusan named Hye Won Yoo, a former medical student, who was paralyzed so badly that he could not even sit up. Yoo both wrote the Principles of this new religion and was the inventor of the air gun which brought prosperity to Moon. Yoo died in 1970.

Moon's followers say that during his stay in Pusan he was extremely busy. During the cold nights he worked on the docks in the dark. During the day when the sun was shining he would pray on top of a hill and receive messages from heaven. From these messages he formulated the *Divine Principle*. They say that he wrote so quickly that the person beside him could not sharpen pencils fast enough.

One of Moon's earliest followers is Duk Moon Aum, now a prominent architect in South Korea. Aum was a friend of Moon while they were classmates in Japan. They also worked together in the Korean student underground Independence movement. Soon after they met in Pusan, Aum became a follower and was the first to call Moon "Sunsaengnim" meaning Master and to relate to him as a revered parent.

In 1952 the first woman to become a follower of Moon was Mrs. Hyun-sil Kang. She was an evangelist in an existing church and a student in a seminary. She had gone to Moon to witness to him but instead became attracted to him and his ideas which were new and surprising. She was deeply involved in the Christian church and valued the Christian teaching so much that she did not accept his words at once. "One time Father [a title for Moon] told her to pray to ask God who is higher, Father or Jesus. . . . By that time she really felt this was not an ordinary teacher;

she was afraid of him, and she followed."[4]

In 1953 Moon went to Seoul. There, in May of 1954, he officially established his new church, calling it in Korean the Tong-il-Kyo and in English the Holy Spirit Association for the Unification of World Christianity (or simply the Unification Church). In 1957 he published the *Divine Principle* and revised it in 1966, the same year he had it published in English in the United States. A revised English edition was published in 1973.

In 1954 Moon's wife of ten years left him because, he claims, "she could not comprehend my mission."[5] Later, on July 4, 1955, in Seoul the police imprisoned Moon and his chief members for three months. His indictment was initially draft dodging but later changed to "communal sex." Most of his followers were men who had left their wives and were part of the new Unification community. Students and professors were expelled from their universities because of engaging in what were called "the scandalous rites of the Unification Church."[6] The charges were dropped, however, and Moon claims to have been persecuted because of the success of his church. His critics say that he was released because of his health which seemed to have been in poor condition at the time.

What were the "rites" which caused so much controversy concerning the early days of the movement? Moon's critics say that he gleaned ideas from Nam Choo Paik whose Theological Mountain at Wensan he had visited prior to 1945. One of the more important ideas was "pikarume" or blood separation, a secret initiation rite. It is said that the female members of the Unification Church had to have intercourse with Moon in order to be purified. Later, intercourse between husbands and wives would purify the male members. Thereafter their offspring would be pure.

The Unification Church in the United States now declares that purification is conferred through Moon symbolically at the wedding ceremony. They fervently deny any promiscuous activities on the part of Moon or any other member of the church. There seems to be no reason to suspect Moon of engaging in the rite since his latest marriage. The early days of the movement, however, leave considerable room to doubt the mere symbolism of the rite.

Moon's married life is also controversial. Koreans refer to it as confusing and strange. Moon claims that he has only married once since his first wife, who failed to become the perfect wife. Others state that he has been married four times. His first wife was Sung Kil Choi, who bore him a son. His second marriage to a Miss Kim is referred to by some Koreans as an arranged marriage. His third wife, Myung Hee Kim, supposedly bore him another son. His fourth (or second) wife is Hak Ja Han, an eighteen-year-old high-school graduate at the time of their wedding in March of 1960. They presently have eight children. Although in 1973 he told followers that his wife had not yet reached his own spiritual perfection, Moon is apparently confident that she will do so eventually.

The union between Sun Myung Moon and Hak Ja Han is called "the Marriage of the Lamb." Moon is called the "Father of the universe" and his wife is called the "Mother of the universe." Consequently their children are considered to be sinless. Together, the parents and their children are heralding the coming perfection of humanity.

Advent in America/   "I did not come for the luxurious life in America,"[7] Moon said to his followers. Rather, according to Moon, God commanded him to go to America to complete the task which Jesus had given him many years before. "I know," said Moon, "I'm destined to fulfill the mission here in America. I'm destined to contribute to the salvation of the world, and America will be my base."[8]

Moon arrived in Los Angeles in December, 1971, to begin his seven-city "Day of Hope" tour across the United States.[9] His first public speaking engagement was in New York in January, 1972. He called Americans to abandon their denominational religions for a real relationship with God through the Second Coming of Christ and to give up their fragmented nationalism

for the building of the Kingdom of Heaven on earth.
Since he can speak little English, Moon delivers his talks in
Korean. His translator is Colonel Bo Hi Pak, nicknamed "God's
Colonel." Occasionally Moon will give a lecture in English, but
he has spoken only in Korean during all of his tours. He is pres-
ently spending some time learning English.

To some, Moon is an engaging speaker, to others obnoxious.
His voice climbs up and down the scale, from high-pitched out-
bursts to guttural roars. His hands and body are in constant
movement while he speaks, jabbing at the air and whirling in
circles. He pounds the podium with his fist and gyrates his head.
But after about twenty seconds he freezes while Col. Pak takes
over. Soon he continues again, then Col. Pak. This rotation goes
on until the end of the sermon.

Before Moon returned to South Korea after his first tour, he
addressed these words to his followers in March, 1972: "I shall
leave America on March 14. I know that there are many young
people who will shed tears upon my departure. However, my
final instruction to them is this: Do not shed tears for me. Shed
your tears and blood for your country, for America. This is my
covenant with you."[10]

The following year in 1973, Moon returned for a twenty-one-
city, "Day of Hope" tour. On this tour in November he said, "I
know that multitudes of lives will depend on me."[11] It was during this second tour that the press became fascinated with Moon
in his support of President Nixon. Three days after this tour
ended, Nixon personally thanked him in the White House on
February 1, 1974. The next month Moon said, "America be-
longs to those who love America the most."[12] Since this is true, he
continued, though a citizen of South Korea, he can claim America as his own.

After a brief working trip to Europe, Moon started his third
"Day of Hope" tour, which covered thirty-two cities in thirty-
two states beginning with Portland, Maine, and speaking twice in
each city. During this tour, Christian groups greeted Moon with
their most vigorous and organized demonstrations denouncing

his claims and doctrines. The tour ended in Honolulu on April 20.

Moon was first admitted to this country in 1972 on a "visitor for business" visa but since then has decided to live in the United States. He and his family are able to remain because of their status as permanent resident aliens, which was granted to them by the Department of Labor. It was on February 26, 1973, that Mrs. Moon received her status because of her petition as a visiting specialist cook. She was sponsored by the Korean Cultural and Freedom Foundation headed by Col. Pak. Soon afterwards she was able to petition successfully for her husband. The immigration official who approved Moon's permanent status was Dale Barton, director of the Washington, D. C., district office. Barton retired in 1973.

Although Moon states that all funds go to the Church and that he uses the funds as befitting its evangelist, he is reportedly worth over $15 million. He is the head of a number of industries in Korea, including the Tong Il Industry Company, the Il Hwa Pharmaceutical Company, the Il Shin Stoneworks Company and the Tong Wha Titanium Company. His various companies produce marble vases, machine parts, ginseng tea, pharmaceuticals, titanium, air rifles and other products. Moon is also financially backed by right-wing Japanese industrialists. The bulk of his wealth, however, comes from his followers, who first give all they own to the Church and then spend the rest of their time in the movement asking for donations or selling various items. A substantial amount collected eventually ends up in Moon's hands or under his direction.[13]

Moon and his family presently reside in Irvington, New York, in a $620,000 estate to which he has added another $50,000 for improvements. He also cruises the Atlantic off Long Island in one of two $250,000 motor yachts. One wonders what Moon's life would be like in America if he had come for "the luxurious life."

THE POLITICAL SETUP

2

THE FEAR OF COMMUNISM HAS OFTEN been used to gain allies and intimidate foes. Reverend Moon has capitalized on this phobia. To Moon, communism is a manifestation of the Antichrist. It is no wonder, therefore, that many people have joined forces with him, ignorant of the battle in which they are actually engaged. Communism is not the issue; it is merely a banner which Moon uses to rally a large enough force to exert a powerful influence on our society. Moon has indeed entered the political arena, and it is here that many people feel he must be challenged in order to be defeated.

The Argument/   The seeds of communism and democracy, Moon says, were in man as far back as the fall. According to the *Divine Principle* (DP 242), Cain was the fruit of Eve's illicit love affair with Satan; later, Abel was the fruit of Eve's love affair with Adam.[1] From then on, the history of man has broken into two lines of philosophy, the lineage of Cain and the lineage of Abel.

Cain as the fruit of the first love symbolized man's relationship with Satan. The political configuration of this relationship has culminated in the form of communism. Abel as the fruit of the second love symbolized man's relationship with God. The political configuration of this relationship has culminated in the form of democracy. Thus, communism is the expression of Satan and democracy is the expression of God.

These two forms of ideologies, however, were not evident to man for many centuries. The first visible sign of communism and democracy did not come until Jesus died on the cross. "The thief crucified on Jesus' right side foreshadowed the democratic world," says Moon, "and the thief crucified on Jesus' left side represented the Communist world."[2] The thief on the left condemned Jesus in Luke 23:39, while the thief on the right defended Jesus in Luke 23:40-41. At that moment the seed was sown so that those on the left would deny the existence of God, such as the communists do today, and those on the right would proclaim the existence of God.

In recent human history communism and democracy have become realities. The world is, more or less, divided between the two. There are some areas in the world where the line of demarcation is so concrete that walls and barbed wires have been constructed as barriers. The Berlin Wall is one. Another is the 38th parallel in Korea, which is the front line for both democracy and communism; and, at the same time, the front line for both God and Satan.

Korea for Moon is more than a spiritual battleground. He says that Korea is the third Israel and will be the place of birth for the coming of the Messiah. Nevertheless, Korea is not so important that it is the nation where God will save mankind. "My followers in Korea bade me farewell in tears," says Moon. "I know there are still many things to do in Korea. But working with only Korea would delay world salvation. America must be God's champion."[3]

God has chosen the United States as the nation around which all other nations are to unite, because the United States is the leading democratic nation and was founded on Christian tenets.

For these reasons, Moon is concentrating most of his efforts on America. "In other words, I am sacrificing all other nations for the purpose of victory in America."[4] Or again, "The movement for world salvation must begin in this country."[5]

Although America is democratic and supposedly Christian and chosen by God, Moon says that she has become self-centered and weary of struggling with communism. "America and her churches are thinking of their own benefits more than God's purpose."[6] Because of widespread disbelief in God, America is plagued with immorality, crime and conflict. She has strayed from the original goals of the pilgrims and our founding fathers. She is desperately in need of help.

Moon says that he has come to bring America back to God and heal her wounds so that democracy can stand strong in the world. According to the *Divine Principle*, democracy is God's political weapon which will annihilate the evil forces of Satan (DP 441-42). "One final war is thus left before us; that is, the war between the ideologies of Democracy and Communism."[7] The defeat of communism, which is the defeat of Satan, will restore the earth back to God and prepare the Kingdom of Heaven on earth for the Lord of the Second Advent.

Korean Oppression/   Two arms of oppression have presently grasped the people of South Korea; one is the iron arm of political tyranny under the dictatorial regime of President Park Chung Hee; the other is the golden arm of religious fanaticism under the spiritual guidance of Sun Myung Moon.

In November of 1972 President Park officially established a new constitution which extended his powers to resemble those of a dictator. Christian leaders, along with others, fervently opposed Park's move and demanded a return to a democratic constitution. On January 8, 1974, Park decreed that anyone who protested against his constitution would be tried, convicted and sentenced for up to fifteen years. On February 1, six Christian ministers and evangelists went to prison because of their criticism of the constitution. They did not have the right of a jury in a civil court. Rather, a special tribunal at the South Korean Defense Ministry judged and sentenced them for up to fifteen years. In April of 1975, Park issued a statement that as long as the communists loom as a threat from North Korea, he must continue his despotic policies for the welfare of South Korea. Among Park's few religious allies in South Korea are Rev. Moon and his Unification Church. Just as the Christian Church has taken an active part in opposing the Park regime, so has Moon taken an equally active part in support of it. Moon has established a training school located just outside Seoul in Soo Taek Ri village, to which the South Korean government annually sends thousands of civilian officials and military personnel for training in the techniques of anti-communism. Moon also heads the International Federation for Victory over Communism, which actively combats communism around the world. Thus, Moon has the favor and support of the government, while at the same time he, as a "religious" leader, lends the administration the aura of respectability.

Communism is the boogieman that Park and Moon constantly employ to arouse fear in the hearts of their countrymen so that they will remain in their protective arms. Tolerating one evil to be rid of a worse one is not so unique. Park does this to maintain his authoritarian rule; Moon does it to allure anti-communist Christians. Both succeed well in camouflaging their dubious activities by creating a subterfuge in their campaign against communism.

Meanwhile the Park regime has created the Korean Central Intelligence Agency (KCIA), an image of the American CIA. The KCIA has been involved in several plots of questionable espionage, such as the abduction in 1973 of Kim Dae Jung (the losing candidate in the 1971 presidential election) from his Tokyo residence and his forced return to Korea where he was jailed. Not known for its subtlety, the KCIA's harassment of Koreans in America became so blatant in 1973 that the State Department ordered an FBI investigation of KCIA activities in the United States. Nevertheless, because of Park's anti-communist stance,

American officials have tended to look away when the rights of South Koreans have been violated.

By 1965, while Moon made his first visit to the United States, his influence in his homeland was strong enough that he was able to have a 45-minute audience with former President Eisenhower. The President agreed to allow his name to be used on the letterhead of the Moon-created Korean Cultural Freedom Foundation, as did Harry S. Truman and Admiral Arliegh Burke. The head of the foundation is Colonel Pak, whom Korean émigrés contend maintains close ties with the KCIA, and whom many others suspect has strong links with the American CIA. Before joining Moon's movement, Pak came to the United States as a military attaché for the South Korean Embassy. According to Philip Agee, an ex-CIA agent and author of *Inside the CIA*, "military attaché" almost always means an "intelligence" man.

Moon and his followers deny any collaboration with Park's government. They contend that to speak out would just lead to a tightening of the screws. It is interesting, however, that Moon's prosperity coincided with Park's military takeover of South Korea. Furthermore, it is commonly understood in South Korea that to have the wealth which Moon has one must be on the most intimate terms with the government.

Nevertheless, if there is any intelligence connection between Moon and the Park regime, it is almost certainly limited to the very top level of the Moon organization and probably involves the organization in lobbying or public relations work for the Korean government and not intelligence collection. FLF (Freedom Leadership Foundation, headed by Moon) Secretary General Gary Jarmin asserts, "Even if Park got more dictatorial, we would support him."[8]

Japanese Connection/ One of the more common stories circulating within the Unification Church is how Moon and other Koreans suffered during the Japanese occupation in World War II. What is not circulated is that President Park himself was an officer in the Imperial Japanese Army during the war and that certain Japanese industrialists who were in part responsible for the repression of Korean Christians are now among Moon's major allies.

Kishi Nobusuke, who was a member of the Imperial Japanese Wartime Cabinet, heads Moon's International Federation for Victory over Communism. He was a Class A war criminal after the war and went on to become Prime Minister of Japan in 1957 through 1961. A close friend of his is Sasagawa Ryoichi, who is the chief financial backer and organizer of the "Genri Undo," a religious organization started by Moon in the 1960s.

Sasagawa was also a former Class A war criminal, who spent time in the Sagumo Prison with Nobusuke. He has long been involved with the Asian Peoples' Anti-Communist League and has played an important role in Japanese politics. With his vast fortune acquired from shipbuilding, gambling and reputed links with organized crime, Sasagawa not only influences the Japanese government but supports Moon's Unification Church. Church officials deny that Sasagawa is actually a member of the Unification Church in Japan, but Col. Pak does admit that Sasagawa is Moon's chief ally in the battle against communism.

The Nixon Ploy/ During the winter of 1973-74 Richard Nixon was acting out the last scenes of an almost Shakespearean tragedy. Once feared ... respected ... hated ... but never before pitied, Nixon was broken in his struggle with himself and with a nation. His downfall was all the more tragic in that during his last days in office his solace should come from Moon.

Moon saw a golden opportunity finally to capture the eyes of the American press by placing himself in the unique position of supporting Nixon. In this he succeeded. He did not succeed in his ploy to unite the nation in love and forgiveness, the theme of his campaign to deter the removal of Nixon from the presidency. Nevertheless, the results of his campaign were amazing.

On November 30, 1973, Moon took time from his second "Day of Hope" tour to issue a statement entitled "Forgive, Love, Unite" to twenty-one major newspapers across the nation. In his comments on the Watergate issue, Moon stated that he had waited for an American to stand up and speak for God concerning the presidency, but none did. Therefore, God spoke to him, and the three key words God imparted were *forgive, love* and *unite*. Furthermore, "The office of the President of the U. S. is . . . sacred," Moon stated. "God has chosen Richard Nixon to be President. . . . Therefore, God has the power and authority to dismiss him."[9]

Beginning on December 1, Moon initiated forty days of prayer and fasting for his members all over the world. Dan Fefferman, a former Berkeley student and anti-war activist, was director of Moon's National Prayer and Fast for the Watergate Crisis. Moon's followers also launched a seven-day public fasting campaign on the Capitol steps as part of the larger forty-day Prayer and Fast. They tried unsuccessfully to organize interfaith support in their behalf.

While demonstrations were conducted across the country and in various parts of the world, six followers of Moon regularly visited congressional offices of both parties, asking the legislators to sign a petition in support of Moon's Watergate "forgiveness" statement. By the end of the year, this effort had been endorsed by four conservative Republican senators (Carl T. Curtis, Hiram L. Fong, Clifford P. Hansen and Strom Thurmond) and twenty-eight congressmen.

On December 11, Nixon sent a statement of appreciation to Moon and the Unification Church for their support. Copies of this statement have been widely distributed by the Church. Two days later in the morning Tricia Nixon Cox and her husband mingled with members of the Unification Church who were demonstrating in support of her father outside the White House. The press gave the occurrence extensive coverage.

That night hundreds of Moon's followers rallied again in front of the White House, bearing signs reading, "Support the President" and "God Loves Nixon." Shortly after 11:00 p.m., the President appeared. Moon's followers knelt down when he came near. And with tears in his eyes President Nixon talked with them for about fifteen minutes.

The following day Moon received an audience with President Nixon. When he met with Nixon, Moon embraced him and then prayed fervently in his native tongue while the President listened in silence. Two days after Nixon resigned, Moon said, "I am sure there is communistic power working behind the scenes. They came to threaten to kill him if he did not resign, and that's what compelled him to do so."[10]

Supporters in Government/ Many political leaders have been listed as supporters of Sun Myung Moon and the Unification Church. So many, in fact, that people have wondered how Moon received their endorsements and whether they are legitimate. Moon essentially has employed three methods in collecting names and has utilized each to its maximum potential.

One method has been the solicitation of proclamations. When he was on his tours, Moon sent runners to state capitols and mayors' offices throughout the country requesting written proclamations which would honor particular days on behalf of Moon and his church. The proclamations are normally signed by the scores with very little scrutiny on the part of governmental officials. Two of the more well-known names to have signed these proclamations, which have been numerously duplicated, were Governor Jimmy Carter of Georgia and Governor George C. Wallace of Alabama.

Another method has been the invitations of prominent figures in government to Moon's speeches on his tours. Many officials either have gone, sent delegates on their behalf or telegrams of best wishes. But once they have done this, their names are frequently used in Moon's public relations materials. Some whose names appear are Senators William L. Scott of Virginia, Jesse Helms of North Carolina, Mark C. Hatfield of Oregon and J. William Fulbright of Arkansas, as well as Mayor John V. Lindsay of New York City and William F. Buckley, Jr.

Then too Moon has been photographed shaking hands with Senators Hubert Humphrey of Minnesota, Strom Thurmond of

South Carolina, James L. Buckley of New York and Edward Kennedy of Massachusetts. The photograph most widely circulated by Moon's followers pictures him with President Nixon. At the time when these methods were being used, little was known of Moon. Consequently, because they thought that he was a Christian evangelist from Korea who denounced communism, they became easy victims. Many of them have long since denounced the movement. Unfortunately the public knows more about their endorsements than their retractions.

Other political figures, however, have defended their endorsements and Moon. In December of 1973 Moon wanted to address a joint session of Congress, but he had to settle for a prayer breakfast at a Washington hotel. A few members of Congress attended. One was Congressman Richard H. Ichord of Missouri, who lavishly praised Moon as a positive force for good and compared the controversy surrounding Moon as similar to that surrounding Christ. Thereafter, his name was listed along with the others mentioned before. When he was confronted with his name being used by the Unification Church, he replied, "I do not wish to be drawn into this controversy but on the other hand I resent anyone telling me that I cannot acquire a meeting place for people who embrace principles and tenets which I admire and respect."[11]

Moon is not one to stand still on past achievements. He also has a lobby in Congress. In 1973 during a New York meeting Moon told his directors, "Master [referring to himself] needs many good-looking girls. He will assign three girls to one senator, that means we need 300. Let them have a good relationship with them. One is for the election, one is to be the diplomat, and one is for the party. If our girls are superior to the senators in many ways, then the senators will be taken in by our members."[12]

Moon's success, however, seems to be more in the House than in the Senate. Although most of Congress have passed it off as either a joke or a bother, House Speaker Carl Albert has been closely linked with female followers of the Unification Church, particularly Susan Bergman. According to Jack Anderson, Sen.

Albert has given them occasional rides in his limousine, helped them move and so forth. Albert denies that they have any political influence on him, although he admits to a pleasant relationship with them.

It is also apparent that elements of the conservative wing of politics are willing to support Moon. Because of his anti-communist line, Moon has found fast friends among prominent conservatives. In *The Right Report* (October 22, 1973) Lee Edwards, famed Reagan biographer, praised Moon's work against communism. Edwards and Allen Brownfeld, a conservative columnist, also have contributed articles to *The Rising Tide*, a newspaper published by the Unification Church.

The Political Arena/   Major periodicals and newspapers have quoted Moon as saying that he will take over the world. "I will conquer and subjugate the world. I am your brain," the *Time* magazine quotes Moon.[14] "The time will come, without my seeking it, when my words will almost serve as law. If I ask a certain thing, it will be done. If I don't want something, it will not be done," the *Chicago Tribune* quotes Moon.[15]

These statements may sound absurd to a casual reader, but an increasing number of parents are beginning to believe them. After joining the Unification Church, many young people have completely severed contact with their families. Naturally parents are alarmed over the situation as they come to realize that the church maintains its members by shielding them from anyone who might be negative toward the church.

With so much publicity focused on Moon's movement, the controversy was bound to enter the political arena of Congress. On February 17, 1976, more than 300 parents from groups throughout the country gathered in Washington, D. C. in an attempt to persuade the government to investigate the Unification Church. Robert Dole, then Republican Senator from Kansas, arranged the conference in a Senate caucus room. The conference grew out of a meeting in 1975 between Dole and one of his constituents, Mrs. Jean Tuttle, a parent whose daughter had previously joined the church.

Spokesmen presented their case to representatives of the Internal Revenue Service, Department of Labor and other agencies. They posed the following questions: Could a movement such as this legally have tax-exempt status? Could it qualify for funding from the Health, Education and Welfare Department? If it is true that Moon's followers are selling flowers on the streets by falsely asserting that the money raised is supporting a drug program, is that illegal? Officials replied that they could not give answers without documentation.

A Dole aid said that the senator is "strongly committed" to the issue but is waiting to see how many parents are concerned before pressing further for governmental action. Dole said that the government should exercise caution in interceding in this matter because "we must be careful to protect the First Amendment guarantee of religious freedom for all Americans."[16]

Some parents told Dole that they are looking for legislative (reform of tax exemption) and judicial (extend parental rights) relief to cope with Moon. They are hoping to secure the help of the American government rather than resort to other methods of rescuing their children from Moon's movement. Meanwhile, they realize that they are confronting a man whose economic and political connections extend from South Korea to Japan to the United States.

11

"AND THEN IF ANYONE SAYS TO YOU,
'LOOK, HERE IS THE CHRIST!'
OR 'LOOK, THERE HE IS!'
DO NOT BELIEVE IT.
FALSE CHRISTS AND FALSE
PROPHETS WILL ARISE
AND SHOW SIGNS
AND WONDERS,
TO LEAD ASTRAY, IF POSSIBLE,
THE ELECT."

(MARK 13:21-22)

THE CHURCH OF MOON'S MAKING

3

INAUSPICIOUS AS THE UNIFICATION CHURCH may have seemed twenty years ago, it is now flourishing throughout the free world. Sun Myung Moon is widely known and followed, even by a number of Americans. There is no disputing the fact that Moon himself made and formed the Unification Church and that no one since its inception has ever challenged his authority from within. The question is whether Moon made his church famous or his church made him famous?

Background/   In May of 1954 Moon officially established the Unification Church in Seoul, Korea. At that time there were five members including Moon. The only person of the five who is still with him is David S. Kim, director of One World Crusade, an affiliate of the Unification Church. Some died, others fell away. There were other members who were in Pusan or Taegu, but they did not participate in forming the association, whose official name is the Holy Spirit Association for the Unification of World Christianity.

Although a Mr. Eu lectured before many people every day on the *Divine Principle*, no one joined Moon's church during the spring and summer of 1954. In October, however, a major breakthrough occurred. One female professor became a member of the church from Ewha Women's University, a Presbyterian college. She was followed by many students and professors from her university and other universities, such as Yonsei University, a men's college. Many current association officials came in at this time, such as Won-jin Hwang, secretary general of the church in Korea, and Young Oon Kim, author of the *Divine Principle and Its Application*.

During this time, controversy surrounded the movement. Five of the professors and students who joined the movement were expelled from Ewha University. Followers of Moon say that it was because they had joined the Unification Church, while others say that it was because they had participated in the sexual practices of the church. In any case, the membership of the church grew regularly and spread throughout South Korea during the late fifties.

The movement soon was extended to Japan where Moon enjoys his second largest following. In 1959, he sent his first missionary, Young Oon Kim, to the United States. The Unification Church currently has headquarters in over 40 nations and followers in over 120 American cities, with Washington, D. C. as its national headquarters.

Although the Unification Church claims to be Christian, it has not been accepted as a member of either the National Council of Churches or the National Association of Evangelicals in Korea, both of whom state that Moon's church is not Christian. "We consider it a pseudo-religion more evil than Satan," said the Rev. Kim Kwan Suk, head of the Korean National Council of Churches.[1]

For the first time in its history, the Council of Churches of the city of New York has rejected an applicant for membership—the Unification Church. The church was twice rebuffed, in January and June of 1975. Serious differences in theology and criticism of some practices of the church were cited by the council's program director, Rev. Franklin Graham, as reasons for the rejection.

The Korean Ministers Association of Greater New York has stated quite unequivocally that Moon teaches a Christian heresy. The Association is comprised of approximately 40 ministers of Korean background who are now working in the metropolitan area. They also represent major denominations, such as the United Church of Christ, United Methodist and United Presbyterian.

The number of adherents within the Unification Church is difficult to estimate. A wide range of sources have claimed that the church has 1 to 2.5 million worldwide, 20-30,000 within the United States and 2-3,000 joining the church per month within this country. The accuracy of any of these figures is impossible to determine.

If we go back to the 1974 claims of the church and compare them with some facts and observations, however, perhaps then we can judge how accurate the 1976 claims are. In 1974 the more conservative estimates of the church listed a following of over a half a million worldwide, with more than 400,000 adherents in Korea, 40,000 in Japan and 10,000 in the United States. All religious groups in Korea are registered at the Ministry of Culture and Public Information. In 1969, the Unification Church registered 900 churches. The "Chong Moo Pillim," their own publication, however, listed 339 churches. Observations estimated that the churches averaged a membership of about 100, which would bring the total membership in Korea to about 35,000. So there seems to be an enormous gap between the 400,000 claimed and the number of those observed.

In Korea the church's membership is no longer increasing because Koreans have become fairly familiar with the doctrines and practices of the organization and no longer are deceived by their methods of proselytizing. It is yet to be seen whether the same will happen in the United States since the church is still growing here. Nevertheless, even the most conservative count cannot be treated lightly. It is reasonable to believe that there are more than 10,000 dedicated core members of the church in the United States. "Thus the Unification Church has more full-time evangelists than any Protestant denomination."[2]

Function/  The emblem of the Unification Church symbolizes the unification of Christianity. The circle in the center represents God, the twelve rays emanating from the center represent the twelve gates to the new Jerusalem mentioned in Revelation 21:10-14 ("On the gates the names of the twelve tribes of the sons of Israel were inscribed. ... And the wall of the city had twelve foundations, and on them the twelve names of the twelve apostles of the Lamb"), and the arrows encircling the symbol represent the universal give and take among God, man and creation that is the basis for harmony and union.

According to information distributed by Moon's followers, the Unification Church is not a church institution nor a Christian denomination, but it is an ecumenical, interfaith movement uniting both Eastern and Western religions. It is a Christian international community of dedicated people building a new world and creating a new culture based on a new morality. Its function is to fulfill the responsibility which Christ shared with his disciples two thousand years ago when he taught them to pray, "Thy Kingdom come, thy will be done, on earth as it is in heaven."

The goals of the church are based on the Unification Principle, which is a guide to the realization of unification on four levels. First is the unification of the mind and heart of the individual centered on God; second, the unification of the Christian community through a common understanding of Christ's message of love and the kingdom; third, the unification of the democratic nations which allow free dialogue and exchange of ideas so that people may come to know the truth, ultimately resulting in a unified, God-centered world of love and brotherhood; and fourth, the unification of science and religion which will lead people to the knowledge of the truth and the Source of Truth. An overview of the progress of the Unification Church since its arrival to the United States seems to indicate an underlying master plan of the church's purposes in this country. Certainly Young Oon Kim came here in 1959 to spread the seeds of her master's teachings. It is also evident that Moon's three national tours from 1972 to 1974 were for the purpose of sowing those seeds, which had been prepared for planting the previous twelve years in major American cities. The years of 1975 and 1976 appear to be a relatively quiet time for the movement, although the mass media has given it considerable coverage. Moon's withdrawal from such activities as in the early seventies has tended to give some people the impression that his religion was merely a spiritual fad that has crested and will soon vanish into oblivion. Careful observers have noted from Moon's talks, however, that now is the period for the church to firmly root itself within our society.

For Moon the critical years are 1977 and 1978. During these years the Unification Church must break ground and begin to grow into a thriving, fruit-bearing organization prepared for the coming of the Lord of the Second Advent. "We are mobilizing thousands of young people in this land, who will go east, west, north, and south to awaken this country to God and stimulate its people into preparing for the glorious day of the new Messiah's coming," said Moon in 1972. "As I declared earlier, the years 1977 and 1978 are most critical. We have launched our movement to be ready for this crisis."[3]

Front Organizations/   Most of the publicity given to the Unification Church from secular or other religious sources has been extremely negative. This publicity also has saturated the major cities and areas of this country. Consequently the followers of Moon have had to form other organizations or programs through which to promote Moon's teachings.

All of these groups have as their ultimate authority Moon. Some are affiliates of others; some are defunct. Although each focuses its attention on particular segments of society, their primary purpose is to serve Moon in his quest for power, whether it be financial, political or spiritual.

The functions of Moon's front organizations have misled many people. The following list will disclose much of this deception which was perpetrated by the followers of Moon. There are so many front groups, however, that only the major ones are included.

Although the Unification Church is clearly a Moon organization, its presidents should be mentioned as well. Neil Salonen, a former engineering student and hospital business manager, is the current president of the American branch of the church. He became a member in 1967, having come from a Lutheran background. Presently in his early thirties, Salonen lives in Washington, D. C., near the national headquarters of the church. He was married by Moon in the famous marriage ceremony in Korea in which Moon presided over 777 couples at one time. Salonen is the recognized spokesman for the church in this country.

Other current presidents are as follows: Young Wei Kim in South Korea, Hideo Oyamada in Japan, Dennis Orne in England, Reiner Vincenz of France and Paul Werner in Germany.

The *Freedom Leadership Foundation* (FLF) is also headed by Neil Salonen and is affiliated with the *International Federation for Victory over Communism* (both founded by Moon). FLF is based in Washington, D. C. and was instituted in 1969. It later matured into the *World Freedom Institute*.

FLF is part of Moon's political arm which promotes various groups against communism. It publishes a weekly newspaper, *The Rising Tide*. A bulk of its energy is spent lobbying on Capitol Hill. An affiliate of FLF is the *Committee for Responsible Dialogue*, which confronts the radical left with debates on college campuses. Another affiliate was the *American Youth for a Just Peace* which supported Administration policy in Vietnam. FLF also sponsored Project Unity and the National Prayer and Fast for the Watergate Crisis (both were to show support for President Nixon).

The *One World Crusade* (OWC) was organized in February of 1972 in the United States and now has branches in Europe and Asia. It has its International Leadership Training Program at the Belvedere Estate in Westchester County, New York. It also prepared the way for Moon's "Day of Hope" tours.

OWC is Moon's evangelistic arm whose stated purpose is to create an ideal world of brotherhood united under God. It is affiliated with the *Council for Unified Research and Education* (CURE), which sponsors annual International Conferences for the Unified Science. Dr. A. Cournand and Dr. John C. Eccles are among some of the Nobel Prize winners who have spoken for the conference. OWC is also affiliated with a Japanese organization, the *International Cultural Foundation* (ICF), which is headed by Osami Kuboki. ICF moved to New York in 1968.

Collegiate Association for the Research of Principles (CARP) is a group which flagrantly attempts to hide its contact with the church. It is philosophical in goals and religious in practice. Better known as CARP, it has a training center on a farm on the Canadian River in Oklahoma and concentrates mostly on the college campuses.

Judaism: In Service to the World lists as its president Dr. Mose Durst. It is also a front for the church in an attempt to attract members of the Jewish community. Like many of its sister organizations, it sponsors concerts and talks geared toward a particular group of people.

The Korean Folk Ballet was started in 1962 and is Moon's national troupe which performs modern adaptations of Korean folk dances around the world. The Little Angels of Korea is its most famous attraction. It is a cultural project of the Unification Church and sponsored by the FLF. They have performed before Queen Elizabeth II in London, President Nixon in the White House and in the General Assembly Hall of the United Nations.

The Little Angels are one of the most effective groups advancing Moon before the public and before dignitaries. *The Rising Tide* wrote, "Tonight the Little Angels will dance and sing their way into your hearts as they have for millions of people around the world in the name of peace and good will. Perhaps as in no other time in history are the words of a great teacher more fitting . . . 'and a little child will lead them.' "[4]

The D. C. Striders Track Club was started by Glenda Moody in Washington, D. C. Moody is their coach and a member of the Unification Church. It also veils its connection with Moon. It has successfully attracted track stars who have won events in major meets. Its honorary chairman is Jesse Owens, who probably does not realize that he is being deceived by Moon.

The *International Pioneer Academy* is in San Francisco but is active throughout the United States. It is employed in training people in leadership roles in the church as well as in world society. The term *pioneers* derives from Moon himself as he labeled his followers the new pioneers in this country.

The *Creative Community Project*, also known as the *New Education Development Systems*, is based in Berkeley, California. It too denies that it is part of the Unification Church, but it is probably the most successful recruitment front for the church.

Other groups are the *International Re-Education Foundation* (based in San Francisco and similar to CARP in function), the *World Federation for Peace and Unity*, the *Professors Academy for World Peace* (based in Seoul and Tokyo), the New Hope Singers International, Sunburst (another musical group), and the *Bi-Centennial God Bless America Committee*, which sponsored Moon's rallies at Yankee Stadium on June 1, 1976, and at the Washington Monument on September 18, 1976.

Financial Power/   Even apart from Moon's own personal fortune in industry, the Unification Church itself is a multimillion-dollar organization. According to *Newsweek*, Neil Salonen stated that the church turned in an $8 million profit for 1974. He has also estimated that contributions run about $6 million annually in this country.

These figures seem extremely small, however, in light of the moneymaking efforts of the Unification members. Former followers have said that they had to work as much as ten to fifteen hours a day, six days a week, selling items or asking donations. Some had to work until a certain amount was achieved; others had to work a specific time-period trying to reach goals of up to and beyond a $1,000 a day. A base of $100 a day is minimum. Even estimating the most conservative of these figures, at $100 a day, five days a week, 10,000 followers would make over $250 million a year in the United States alone. And this does not include the value of all the possessions new converts give to the church.

It is easy to understand, therefore, how the Unification Church can own thousands of acres of American land valued in the several millions. Among their major pieces of property is their seminary in Dutchess County near the Hudson River. Formerly the Christian Brothers monastery, the 255-acre estate in Barrytown, New York, was purchased for $1.5 million and is now used as a training center. Church property also includes the Belvedere estate in Tarrytown, N. Y., reportedly at a cost of $850,000, which will be part of the church's university, and a 22-acre estate in Irvington, N. Y., reportedly at a cost of $620,000, which serves as a home for Moon and his family. In addition to its New York properties, the church owns 650 acres in Booneville, California (which operates as the West Coast training center and is called International Ideal City), and their office building off Dupont Circle (which is their national headquarters in Washington, D. C.).

The potential wealth of the Unification Church is enough to stagger the imagination. Nevertheless, what income the church nets through fundraising and what properties and corporations it possesses, which are acknowledged by the movement, are sufficient to testify to the financial power of Rev. Moon. If his Unification Church fades away, it will not be for lack of funds. Rather, money may be the most important factor in keeping the church alive.

THE UNIFIED FAMILY

4

WITHIN THE PAST DECADE THE FAMILY UNIT in our society has rapidly disintegrated. The Unification Church has taken full advantage of this situation. In fact a key to their success has been their own family oneness in contrast to the breakdown of the American family. The Unified Family, as they are often referred to, is also so isolated that it seems to exist outside the framework of our society. So it is that their unity and seclusion are essential both to their appeal and to their preservation.

The Family/ The Family is comprised mostly of young people in their twenties and thirties, an ideal age for maximum energy and dedication. Although some of them have previously been married and have joined with or without their mates, a majority are singles whose only responsibility is to the church. The Family is a potpourri of people from all racial and social backgrounds with a slight emphasis on the educated. Women are on an equal level with men, although none hold outstanding official positions. Nevertheless, women such as Young Oon Kim and

Onni Soo Lim Durst, have a strong voice in the movement. Generally members of the Family have had some type of contact with Christianity; their understanding of it, however, has been flexible enough to be converted into Moon's theology.

People have become Family members from a variety of circumstances. But most of the members share one or more of these characteristics. They (1) are in search of an authority figure in their lives; (2) are alienated from their families and society; (3) have recently experienced an emotional trauma; (4) are attracted to an idealistic philosophy complete with absolutes; (5) have a background in a dead church that makes them vulnerable to and hungry for spiritual experiences; or (6) are newly converted to Christ and have had little or no biblical training and accept the doctrines of the Unification Church as true Christianity.

Many young people are seeking authority in their lives, because they lacked that authority as they grew up. Perhaps, because of death or divorce or even passivity on the part of fathers, this problem has emerged in many families in our present society. The result has been a cultural youth-quest for a father-figure in their lives.

Sun Myung Moon is the "perfect Father" to those in search of one. They not only are in total submission to his authority, but they refer to him as Father. The doctrines and religious practices of the church all substantiate this role-playing so that even their individual salvation depends on Moon as Father and his wife as Mother in giving them birth into the Kingdom of Heaven. With so much love and trust placed on their newly acquired father, it is no wonder that their original families have little influence on them. Meanwhile, the Unification Church has had the most difficulty with those converts who have a close relationship with their fathers.

One needs to look no further than philosophy and literature to realize that people have never been more alienated from themselves and their society. With families being shattered and the concept of marriage being disputed, one cannot find security and comfort even in the family unit. Indeed people have become islands separated by a dark and turbulent ocean with the constant fear of being flooded and lost in that ocean forever. The Unified Family eagerly welcomes anyone to become an intimate member of their family. And to those who are fearful, that temptation is almost impossible to resist. The camaraderie of brothers and sisters living together, working together and worshiping together binds them into a family unity few families ever achieve. The unification goals of the church solve the problem of alienation in theory, but in practice it may be an even greater problem for many to reconcile their total break from family and friends.

Few people have the character strength to experience an emotional crisis in their lives and walk in control of their emotions. Most young people who have been initiated into the painful experience of romantic disappointment have not only had their hearts crushed but have stepped from the youthful world of innocence and ignorance to the adult world where reality can be terribly cruel. The predicament of coping with one's needs in a world full of anguish and sorrow has led many people to seek relief any way possible.

The Unification Church gives relief to hurting people in two very important ways. First, since the movement carefully manipulates hearts to be completely devoted to Moon, painful emotions are systematically rechanneled into a love for the Family and Moon. Second, romance is forbidden in the movement and marriages are arranged by the leaders. Lives are so regulated that there is little fear of unsuccessful relationships and much security in the hope of a predetermined marriage. Nevertheless, a number of those who have left the Family have left in pairs because they had fallen in love.

Rationalism, situation ethics, liberal theology, existentialism, Eastern mysticism and occult philosophy have all contributed to the collapse of social acceptance of absolute truths. Living in a world of relativism presents many problems, but foremost is the problem of anxiety. Self-identity is either lost in a myriad of particulars or in the oneness of everything. Absurdity has replaced idealism, and the world is bereft of noble truths.

The *Divine Principle* and the inner teachings of the Unification Church provide people with all the absolutes anyone could ever want. Not only is the religious philosophy of the Family absolute at every point, but it is idealistic as well. Every question is answered, all of life's riddles are solved by this super-spiritual structure. Furthermore, individual identity is assimilated into the identity of the Family which proclaims love and fraternity to the world—an ideal that gives anyone dignity. Although the doctrines of Moon are orchestrated to control the thoughts and the will of his followers, many minds have been devastated because of the strange quality of the spiritual teachings of the church. These, however, we will deal with in Part Three.

The Christian church today has become so culturally oriented that spiritual experiences often are not only lacking but are condemned. A number of young people, therefore, are leaving their congregations and are experimenting with drugs and Eastern mysticism in their quest for an experiential spirituality. As long as "Christian" congregations present a God who is way out there somewhere, if there at all, their youth are going to be left dissatisfied and thirsting for a more personal relationship with God.

The beliefs and practices of the Unification Church afford their members plenty of spiritual experiences. Religious inspiration and joy, never before felt, swell the hearts of many believers. The Family stresses a devotion to a personal God, not to an impersonal concept. Thus, fervent zeal to serve God spurs many people who have fled from the apathetic atmosphere of a dead church. The Family also encourages intimate contact with the spirit world, as we will see in chapter 7.

Many young people have realized that Christ alone is the answer to their needs and to their problems and have accepted Jesus as their Savior. Some have been drawn to this commitment by reading the Bible; others have been witnessed to by Christians. But some of these young Christians who do not find a church home and have not developed a biblical foundation for their faith are ready to listen to any church which declares Jesus as the Messiah.

Probably this set of circumstances snares more people into the Unified Family than any other. The Family is more than willing to teach a young Christian what it feels is the truth, and because they employ Scriptures to back their arguments, their doctrine is easily accepted by those who have had little or no biblical training. Furthermore, the Family frequently lauds the life of Jesus and refers to the Family members as Jesus' true followers. After joining the Family, however, these new members soon realize that there is someone more important than Jesus. And, more often than not, they come to accept Sun Myung Moon as the Messiah.

The Marriage Sacrament/   The religious practices of the Unification Church are few and simple. The Family employs little ritual in their services and worship. They concentrate on group praying, singing and the sermons. Christian sacraments such as baptism and the Lord's Supper are not practiced. Furthermore, church leaders are not ordained.

Although the Family has the veneer of a Christian church, they consider baptism and communion as practices of a previous dispensation much as Christians consider Jewish practices as being under the Old Testament dispensation. When they attend Christian churches in order to recruit, however, they will partake of communion. Nevertheless, the only rite which can be called a sacrament in the church is marriage.

Unification weddings and marriages are actually a part of the doctrine of salvation. Marriage is believed to be essential to salvation because God formed man in two images of himself—male and female, and together they represent God totally. Thus, "only married members will enter the Kingdom of God."[1]

Preceding the sacraments is belief. In the Christian church it is belief in Jesus Christ; in the Family it is belief in Sun Myung Moon. Ken Sudo explains this in the *120-Day Training Manual,* a book employed to train people in the Unification Church to become leaders in the movement. He says, "By loving the Messiah [Moon] and obeying and believing the Messiah more than my own life, and by doing what he requires with great faith, now we can realize the Kingdom of God on earth and in heaven."[2] "We must clearly understand the difference between the Unification Church and the Christian Church. . . . Father [Moon] is sinless, Mother [Moon's wife] is sinless, and their children are sinless. This is called the Messiah's family; this was established in 1967, on December 31. The sinless family was established on earth."[3]

The training manual further states, "This is salvation, Unification Church. Through Father [Moon] and Mother [his wife] we can be born anew, sinlessly. . . . Father is given authority here on earth by God to forgive sins."[4] Essentially this rebirth and forgiveness occurs through belief, dedication and marriage in the Family.

Marriage, however, is not easily attained. There is no dating. As a matter of fact romance is strictly forbidden. It is customary for an individual to reach conditional perfection before being qualified for marriage in order to have a sinless marriage and sinless children, and this normally takes about three years.

God must approve all marriages in the church, but God is invisible. Therefore, the Messiah (Moon) must approve them. In the early years when there were fewer members, Moon himself arranged the marriages. Now, because of the large number of followers, marriages are arranged by senior members of the Family and approved by Moon. Ordinarily "both men and women submit lists of five candidates and after counseling, their leaders make a choice."[5] There are exceptions. For example, Moon permitted Onni Soo Lim to bypass the rules and choose Mose Durst for her spouse because of her great success in recruiting people.

The Family defends its practices by saying that the cause for the disintegration of the American family unit has been marriages formed from selfish desires and not based on God's will. They also say that brothers should love all sisters equally and vice versa so that any brother can marry any sister with the highest purity of love.

A Unification wedding is a holy wedding which supposedly purifies the blood. The wedding is public and preceded by a wine ceremony which is not public. The wine is believed to be a symbol of pure blood.

Moon is the only person who has performed the weddings, although the time will come when heads of families will do it. Mass marriage ceremonies originally catapulted Moon to fame in the United States. Each time the number of participants has increased. In February of 1975, Moon married eighteen hundred couples in Seoul, Korea, from twenty-five countries, including seventy couples from the United States.

After the wedding, couples must refrain from sex for at least forty days in line with biblical references to fasting. Even after the celibate periods, couples tend to live as brothers and sisters in the Family, so that independent family units cannot be formed to "threaten the cohesiveness of the communal family and the authority of its leader."[6] Nevertheless, married couples in the Family are taught to have many children in order to multiply the Messiah's family.

Couples or individuals, who were married outside of the church, are not recognized as married in the eyes of God. Ken Sudo states, "Even marriage which has nothing to do with God must be denied once and must be started anew."[7] Couples married before joining the Family must undergo a period of separation and live as brother and sister for six months or more. Later they can resolemnize their vows in a Family rite.

Fornication and adultery are sins worse than murder. Fornication is believed to be the root of sin. It is against God and because of it man lost God. It is also against marriage and the union of man with the Messiah. There can be no greater sin than this in the Family.

Political Power/   "Father [Moon] shed blood for me to be blessed. He sacrificed his life and gave me life. My life came from

Father, from the True Parents. Without Father, there is no life. Father is more precious than myself, than even all mankind."[8]

These words from the *120-Day Training Manual* exemplify the deep devotion and dedication members of the Family have for Moon. They also reveal something of the technique the church employs to rouse the hearts of his followers. The Family is taught that Moon suffered greatly in his struggles with Satan and that he suffered for every believer. Furthermore, through his spiritual warfare with Satan he secured victory and finally subjugated Satan. Because of his sinless life and his victory, Moon can give life to his believers, a life not even Jesus can give, for Moon has established the physical Kingdom of Heaven on earth.

The key to winning a member's love for Moon is to show how much Moon loves that individual, and that love is most evident in his sufferings. That is why so much emphasis is placed on Moon's suffering at the hands of the communists. But there is also a pain which transcends ordinary life. A pain which only Moon can feel as the Messiah. A pain which binds each follower to Moon. A pain which is like a ball and chain to keep a person enslaved. "Therefore, however miserable you may feel, however sad you may feel, crying and shouting because of misery and sadness, still just in front of you is Father and he is experiencing even deeper misery and grief and despair."[9]

The Family is used to benefit Moon in many ways: wealth, property, fame, religious self-glorification and political power. Perhaps the most disturbing of all is political power. Moon is a man extremely interested in controlling the political destiny, first of the United States and then of the world, and he makes no attempt to disguise his ambitions.

What Moon essentially says is that Christianity has lost the spiritual force to save this world. As a matter of fact Christianity betrayed the Lord of the Second Advent and consequently Korea is a divided country. The Family is taught that the true boss of Satan's dominion is Kim Il-sung, head of North Korea, and that America must suffer now because of her disobedience to God's will when she lost Nixon. Since America is Christian, the destiny of the world will be decided on whether America and Christianity will belong to God or Satan. Of course, there is only one way to God. "America must come back to God. The only decision is to obey God to obey God's words. And God's words come through Rev. Moon."[10]

Still, it is not a matter of America and Christians realizing this and turning to Moon. Moon knows that it may well take political persuasion to steer the course of history in the direction of his desire. "If the U. S. continues its corruption and we can find among the senators and congressmen no one really usable for our purposes, we can make senators and congressmen out of our members."[11]

Here is where the Family can be of most use to Moon. Already they have a lobby in Washington, a political newspaper and political organizations. It would not be so remarkable for a Family member with his total dedication and Moon's financial backing to fill a political office. "We can make senators and congressmen out of our members," says Moon. "Let's say there are five hundred sons and daughters like you in each state; then we could control the government."[12]

To counter attacks from his critics, Moon utilizes political tactics as well. Those who condemn him, his movement or organizations are labeled communists. For example, the Spiritual Counterfeits Project (SCP) in Berkeley, California, is an archnemesis of Moon. The SCP sends people and literature throughout the United States revealing the esoteric teachings and practices of the Unification Church. Meanwhile, the Unified Family has been telling people that the SCP is a communist organization and that is why it is opposed to Moon. In fact the SCP is a Christian ministry which is as anti-communist as it is anti-Moon.

Nevertheless, the most frightening aspect of Moon's potential political power is his power over his followers. Not only would they become political leaders for him, but many have said that if Moon ordered them to take up arms (which, by the way, he manufactures) and fight the communists in Korea, they would do so. This may sound incredible, but only to those who have not heard the testimonies of those who have left the movement. Moon, of course, encourages such commitment:

Don't rely on your own power. Unless you become one with the True Parents, in no way will power flow into you. So this is the one basic and fundamental condition. . . . You are to become a core soldier of the True Parents. . . . Your whole body, every cell of your body, every movement, every facial motion, even every piece of hair, every ounce of energy, must be directed to this one point. Those who have developed that attitude, to live or die, must make it go.[13]

THE CONVERSION

5

THE CONVERSION INTO THE UNIFICATION CHURCH is probably the most controversial issue in the news media concerning Sun Myung Moon. In 1974 Moon stated, "I truly disciplined and set the traditions of our movement in Korea, so that they [Moon's followers] were completely liberated from the fear of how to live, what to eat, and how to sleep."[1] These are powerful words and they raise the question: What induces people to surrender their lives wholeheartedly to Moon? Is it brainwashing, mind control, mind manipulation or behavior modification? Could it be "heavenly indoctrination" or simply total faith in Moon and his ideas? An overview of a person's encounter with, acceptance of and life in the Unification Church or its many front organizations may help us discover why so many young people have chosen a lifestyle which seems so incredible to so many others.

The Encounter/ The followers of Moon you are most likely to encounter are young people, a majority of whom are in their twenties. They are well-groomed and polite. They dress simply and wear little or no makeup. Short-haired young men and young women in neat, modest skirts and dresses give a clean-cut, conservative image. Their most striking characteristic, however, is their smiles. That is a key to winning you to their movement.

Although most of their proselytizing takes place on college campuses, you may find them at shopping centers, libraries, airports or wherever a mass of people are. Their primary aim is to persuade you to accept an invitation to their center for dinner.

They may employ any one of several lines of persuasion, depending upon your beliefs and personality. Generally anything you say you are into, they will say they are into. Their common line, however, is that they are in a movement which is unifying the peoples of all races and beliefs around love and fraternity. They will insist that they are offering a way of life and not a religion. They invite you to their center where you can see people from many different backgrounds and cultures demonstrate their love and where you can hear how they hope to achieve this goal.

If you fail to accept their invitation, then their secondary aim is to obtain your name and phone number. Later they may telephone you as much as three to five times a day for a month. Some people go just to stop their persistent calling.

When you attend their dinners, you are requested to remove your shoes and again you are met with smiles. Two sets of people are present: the followers of Moon and those who have been invited like yourself. Some of the followers circulate among the guests and others are assigned to a specific guest. You are often complimented on your looks, pesonality, dress or whatever. Most importantly, they want to impress upon you that they love you. Along with the meal, you are introduced to a speaker who gives a set lecture about the problems and needs of the world and how they are building a community based on universal love. Sometimes a speaker will also discuss mankind's scientific ability to create an ideal world, further stating that only a God-centered technology can truly satisfy every person's desire for material happiness. Moon is rarely mentioned either at the first encounter or here at the dinner.

While you eat with them, listen to their lectures and prayers, and share in their singing, you again notice their constant smiles. You may also wonder why they never give you an opportunity to withdraw and reflect upon what is happening. The former is making a deep impression on you; the latter you pass off as their concern for you.

Finally they ask you to attend a workshop. Workshops last three, seven, twenty-one, forty or one hundred-and-twenty days, but the one to which they normally invite you first is the three-day workshop. Depending on the area of the country, the workshop may be located at a church, a house, an estate, a camp, a rural retreat (such as Booneville, California) or a training center (such as Barrytown, New York). The shorter ones are designed to get you committed, the longer ones train you to be a leader. In any case, their invitation is extremely alluring.

The Three-Day Workshop/ By the time you reach their workshop, you will realize that the followers of Moon regard each other as "Family." Soon you will also realize that you are spoken of as a "spiritual child" and that the people who brought you are alluded to as "spiritual parents."

It becomes immediately apparent to you that you are not to be left alone and that all "spiritual children" have someone of the opposite sex from the Family assigned to them. If you should wander off by yourself, someone will follow you and politely ask you to rejoin the group. You are even escorted to the rest room.

You also learn that there is a rigidly held schedule. There are specific times for eating, exercising, playing, singing, listening to lectures and discussing them. You are separated into small groups, led by a team leader who has to have perfect control, not approximate control. From the beginning, the leader directs his or her group like a kindergarten teacher, telling you when to do this or that.

Family members are to assist the leader and respond perfectly to what they are asked to do. They are to set an example for you. If their enthusiasm or diligence slackens, they are taken aside or handed notes and sternly reprimanded.

Sharing is programmed for you to speak on spiritual things. Rarely are you permitted to engage in casual conversation with anyone. Even while you are eating, your leader either talks or calls on someone to share so that there is little opportunity for personal dialogues.

Twice a day you play a physical sport such as dodgeball. Squads of players are formed, and you chant and cheer with the rest of your teammates. You feel a unity with them and a release of aggressions and tensions which have been building up.

Creativity is taunted and you see only conformity. Unless you are carefully searching for contradictions, you are not aware of them in the training sessions, because the pressures to conform are so inherent and so subtle.

All day you are bombarded by ideas and concepts. There is little relaxation, and so your resistance is low. When you refrain from sharing or resist in any way, you are met with benevolent concern. Peer approval is an important technique which subtly tells you to conform. The Family members aim directly at your most vulnerable points: the need to belong, to feel useful and to feel loved. Throughout the workshop you are flooded with affection—hugs, pats, hand-holding and smiles.

There comes a point when negative reaction to the regimental control gives way to automatic reaction, and you then try to please. But, you quickly learn that the only way to please is to conform. Furthermore, your intellectual objection is being undercut by means of emotional seduction. You succumb many times to small acts of conformity without realizing it. You feel guilty when you hold back, and you are told that wanting to be alone is a symptom of fear and alienation. You also note that the lectures are becoming more and more emotional and that you are being infected by them.

It is at this point that you are asked to join their movement or the Family. The member who has been with you the most will beg and plead with you to stay. There will even be tears along with the promises. They will continue to implore until you decide to join.

Family Lifestyle/   After committing yourself to the movement, things will begin to change; but first, they give you about two weeks of adjustment. They call it "losing," a period when your desires become nothing. It is based on the philosophy of giving to others. During this time, you are expected to give all your possessions to the movement. Normally you return home once to claim your belongings, if they are of any value. You may even take a few other items.

During this one visit home, you may be accompanied or tailed by a Family member, who is called a "shadow." Henceforth, your communications with your physical family will be mostly through correspondence which will become less and less. The church sees to it that being with them makes you so vulnerable and so unable to cope with the real world that you are compelled to stay with them. When you do step out into the world, it is a shock—a cultural shock.

You are taught that everyone not in the movement is under the influence of Satan and that you should mistrust them. They insist that the devil works strongest through those closest to you to destroy your faith. This naturally offsets the concern of parents and friends, most of whom want you to leave. You are told that their motivation is love, but because love in the world is fallen, they cannot understand that their motivation is evil. If someone talks to you from outside the Family, no doubt they are trying to take your mind away. You begin to fear the world and those in it. Thus you become dependent on the group for love and positive reinforcement. After alienation is complete, you are told that you can leave if you want.

You are required to adhere to a schedule more demanding than the workshop's. You sleep five or six hours a day. Your diet consists of starchy foods, low in proteins. Often you must fast for many days; there was, for example, a forty-day fast for Nixon. You must fundraise. You must recruit. Everything is long . . . long prayer meetings, long days of fasting, long working days.

You sing and pray before meals, before classes, before work, before evening get-togethers. Most songs are traditional or Korean hymns. There are also many old campfire songs such as "You Are My Sunshine" and "This Land Is Your Land." You pray in groups out loud, and when you are alone, you find yourself saying the same words. There is a great emphasis on repetition. You repeat things over and over again, and you do it hypnotically.

Alcohol and drugs are forbidden. You must also learn to abstain from tobacco. Fornication is the worst possible sin. Rules are strict, but there are four annual holidays for the Family: Parents' Day, Children's Day, World Day and God's Day.

If your body reacts negatively with illness or fatigue, it is a sign of Satan invading your body. If you begin to work less, they say you are being selfish and not growing close to God. If you object to their rules, they say it is Satan working through you against God.

You are taught to mistrust your mind. You are given an interpretation for every situation. You no longer need to think or evaluate for yourself but, instead, recall what was told you for that situation. Finally, they say that if you leave you will die spiritually and be possessed by Satan physically.

You become so dependent that you will do anything for them and for Moon.

The Messiah Is Moon!   By now you have been familiarized with Moon and his doctrines. You are constantly praying and studying the *Divine Principle*. You are discouraged from reading anything else unless it pertains to Moon. When you read newspapers or other writings, you are told that it is a selfish thing to do because it is something you want to do. Instead, they tell you that reading the *Principle* will bring you closer to God.

The primary function of the lectures on the *Principle* is to keep you from thinking about anything other than what they are trying to teach you. If your mind wanders or you fall asleep, they throw things at you or abruptly yell, "Pay attention!" You are told, "Twenty-four hours a day our feelings should be concentrated on Father and Mother."[2]

The more you learn, the more there is to learn. The advanced courses are held at the seminary in Barrytown, where you learn to become a leader. Moon has set three standards for you and others to be a leader in his organization: First, you must be a good speaker; second, you must be a good public relations man; and third, you must make money.[3]

You realize that there is a difference between what is taught in the church and what teachings are projected to the public. You may notice that the church is telling Christians that the Unification Church is trying to unify Christianity and that followers of Moon are Christians. What you are taught, however, is that Christianity has failed God, and because it has betrayed the Lord of the Second Advent, Christianity must obey the Unification Church to return to God.

The greatest difference, however, is their teaching concerning Moon. Only in the church is Moon spoken of as the Messiah and the Lord of the Second Advent. "Therefore, life in the Unification Church is far different from Christian life or life in the Old Testament Age—because we have the Messiah living with us."[4] "Then they can understand that Rev. Moon is Messiah, Lord of the Second Advent."[5]

No longer is Christ to be thought of as Savior and Lord. To Moon alone belong these titles. You speak of Moon as Master or Father. Through him God has imparted revelations revealed in the *Divine Principle* and the *Master Speaks*, Moon's esoteric teachings. Moon is the one who has finally decoded the Bible. Moon and his wife are the Perfect Parents who will bring physical salvation to you and the world. You even must pray through them. "Prayer should be offered to Heavenly Father through True Parents."[6]

Furthermore, you are taught to have a personal relationship with Moon and his wife. "When Father trained us, Father said at one point that the sisters could fall in love with Father and think of him in a romantic way as well as our Father and that the brothers should think of Mother in a romantic way. He said we could feel a closer bond through that and could somehow live in an intoxicated state thinking about our True Parents."[7]

You are told, "Unless people can understand Father is the Messiah, they cannot move in."[8] To you Moon is everything.

Fundraising/   To belong to the Unification Church you must be a fundraiser. So you are out for long hours in any weather conditions, asking for donations or selling flowers, candy or other items, any way you can for Rev. Moon and his movement. You are told that Moon cannot live in rags and hope to influence people like the Rockefellers. You are also told that the movement needs money in order to fulfill the purpose of creation.

You are taught that, since Satan deceives God's children, you are justified in deceiving Satan's children in accordance with God's will, a doctrine known as "heavenly deception," which gives you the right to say anything you want to people outside the Family. You can tell them that the money will be used to help the emotionally retarded or drug victims or wayward kids. You know, however, that the church has no such programs. Saying that you are working for a drug rehabilitation program is especially successful with old people. And when the church is approached about this practice, officials deny that deceit is used. If it does occur, they say it is due to overzealousness of individual followers.

Although you and your brothers and sisters in the Family live on very little, you know that Moon lives in opulence. But that's fine with you, since "Everything must be offered to Father first, then we are qualified to use it."[9] Thus you make money for Moon. But you also do so because the amount you make in a day depends on how spiritual you are. So you struggle to be as spiritual as everyone else.

Fundraising becomes almost an obsession with you. You and your house or region are constantly told to make a certain quota.

You are goaded by such words as, "In this age it is far more important to ask than to pray. . . . So to be very precious, Father's words must be far better than this commandment. . . . We cannot understand the value of Father's words. 'Pray, make money.' This is better than the Ten Commandments."[10]

Finally, since money is part of creation, it too must have joy in being one with God. And the only way for it to return to God is through Moon. So it is your responsibility to make as many bills happy as possible. "Do you like to make green bills happy? When green bills are in the hands of fallen men, can they be happy? Why don't you make them happy? So many green bills are crying. Have you ever heard them crying? Not yet? You must hear. They are all destined to go to Father. This is our responsibility. Eventually, unless everything goes through Father, it cannot be happy. . . . When Jesus came He couldn't fulfill the second blessing, so he wasn't fully qualified to have dominion over the creation and restore things. Christians think that the Messiah must be poor and miserable. He did not come for this. Messiah must be the richest."[11]

Kidnapping and Deprogramming/   You frequently hear complaints against Moon and the Unification Church, that the church is kidnapping young people such as you. But you know, since the church has made you well aware, that it is the parents and their confederates who are the real kidnappers and that many of your brothers and sisters in the Family have been tricked by their folks and forced to undergo physical and psychological brainwashing, which they call deprogramming.

The church itself is accused of brainwashing its members, but you know that it isn't true because you know that you are not brainwashed. The church has also been accused of violence, drugging food and other such acts, but either you have not been aware of them or you believe that, if they did occur, they were necessary for the good of the movement. Besides, how can anyone condemn the church when it makes every attempt to dispel the fears of parents. Haven't Farley Jones, Bob Heater and other

Family leaders initiated parent programs which work through legal channels and the media to inform families of their children's roles in saving the world? Haven't your parents been invited to the center to see for themselves how happy and how fulfilled your life is? And aren't the desires of the church to have everyone come to know the New Truth and "Then we can swallow up each entire family."[12]

Nevertheless, parents still object to the church and many have become bitter enemies, such as Maurice Davis, a New York rabbi on the East Coast, and Daphne Greene, a San Francisco socialite on the West Coast. There are even groups such as the Citizens Freedom Foundation (P. O. Box 256, Chule Vista, CA 92010), Citizens Engaged in Reuniting Families (252 Soundview Ave., White Plains, NY 10606) and Return to Personal Choice (1400 Commonwealth Ave. W., Nexton, MA 02167).

Most of the parents, however, who are disturbed over the situation say in frustration, "We didn't take her (or him) out by force because we could have gotten her out bodily but not mentally—she would just run away, back to them." But many parents lure their children away to be confronted with a deprogrammer, whom they hired to psychologically break the Family's hold on them.

There are three principal deprogrammers in the country, and demand for their services is heavy as growing numbers of parents try to pull their children out of the Unification Church. The best known is Ted Patrick, a one-time community relations officer of former California Governor Ronald Reagan. The Family refers to him as "Black Lightning" or the "Black Devil." You are made to fear him as you would Satan himself. The other two deprogrammers are a father-and-son team from Columbus, Ohio, Joe Alexander and Joe Jr. All three went into business because they had relatives who became involved in cults.

You are told that the deprogramming sessions often last for days, during which time people are kept awake, given little to eat, are constantly questioned and ridiculed for their belief in the church. You are told that Satan is behind the deprogramming, trying to destroy your faith and take over your will. The deprogrammers say that all they do is to show the conflict between Moon's teachings and the Bible.

You know that many have left the church because of the deprogramming, and some are even working against the church. Nevertheless, you know that there are two weaknesses in deprogramming: One is that many deprogrammers not only turn you off to Moon and the Unification Church but they turn you off to Christianity as well, telling you to stay away from the whole religious trip; the other is that many people who have been deprogrammed are left with a void in their lives. Meaning has been taken out of your lives and nothing was put in place of it. Consequently, after awhile you return to the church even more dedicated than before.

Recruiting/   Daily life in a Family house is a totally regulated training process designed to lead each individual to the perfect state, to provide monetary support for the movement and to win converts. You achieve conditional perfection in a period of about three years. True perfection takes many, many years. When conditional perfection is attained, you are entitled to marry a perfect mate chosen by the church. For then you will have a sinless marriage with sinless children.

An additional rule is that in order to become perfect you must receive Moon's blessing. To do so you must bring three "spiritual children" into the church. Then you can get married. It is extremely important for you to marry because marriage is essential for your complete salvation.

Objects are often termed "Holy," such as the "Holy Rock," a rock where followers kneel in prayer because Moon frequently stands on it to preach in Barrytown. In order to witness you must sanctify a central place for praying. This place is called the "Holy Ground," and is holy until you leave. "Holy Salt," which was made when Moon married, is that which makes a particular place holy. Once you have established a "Holy Ground" you can start to witness, assured that God is directing and anointing you.

Soon you are in the streets searching for potential converts. You are told that the college campuses are especially ripe with vulnerable people during final exams when students are emotionally depressed. You look for young people in a crisis period or a transition in their lives. You want to convert high quality people for the church, and that is another good reason why you like to witness at the universities.

You are told that dead churches also have many vulnerable people and that this is called "infiltration." You especially want to emphasize love to them, and not truth. You are eager to invite people to the center and your face wears a big smile.

111

"AND HE SAID TO THEM,
'O FOOLISH MEN,
AND SLOW OF HEART TO BELIEVE
IN ALL THAT THE
PROPHETS HAVE SPOKEN!
WAS IT NOT NECESSARY THAT
THE CHRIST SHOULD SUFFER
THESE THINGS AND ENTER
INTO HIS GLORY?'
AND BEGINNING WITH MOSES AND
ALL THE PROPHETS,
HE INTERPRETED TO THEM IN ALL
THE SCRIPTURES THE THINGS
CONCERNING HIMSELF."

(LUKE 24:25-27)

THE PRINCIPLE

6

ALTHOUGH OTHER UNIFICATION DOCUMENTS play important roles in the movement, the *Divine Principle* contains the basic tenets and doctrines of the Unification Church. Family members believe that God has imparted revelations to Moon and that most of these are disclosed in the *Divine Principle*. "With the fullness of time, God has sent His messenger to resolve the fundamental questions of life and the universe. His name is Sun Myung Moon" (DP 16).

The Completed Testament/ The *Divine Principle* serves a twofold purpose: It indoctrinates adherents of the Unification Church into a particular line of belief and it undermines all forms of present New Testament theology, particularly evangelical, fundamental Christianity. It is also an eclectic blend of Oriental thought and Christian theology. Converts are continuously instructed on it so that it becomes their bible. Just as Jews refer to the Scriptures, Moslems refer to the Koran, Hindus refer to the Vedas, so in like manner the Unification Family refers to the *Divine Principle*. For them it is the present truth and super-sedes Christian theology.

Moon breaks history into three stages. The period from man's fall to Christ's coming he calls the Old Testament age, the period from Christ to the coming of the Lord of the Second Advent is the New Testament age and the period from the Lord of the Second Advent onward is the Completed Testament age. It is understandable, therefore, why the *Divine Principle* is called the Completed Testament. Each stage is a growth in man's under-standing of God's truth. In each age God dispenses only that much truth which man can grasp. Presently man has spiritually matured to a level where all truth can be revealed. Thus God has employed Moon to disclose the Completed Testament.

Christians will not be pleased to hear that new revelations of truth have appeared, since they believe that the Bible is perfect and absolute in itself. The Bible according to Moon, however, is "not the truth itself, but a textbook teaching the truth"; it must not be regarded as "absolute in every detail" (DP 9). Neil Sa-lonen, president of the American branch of the church, ex-plains, "No Christian on earth understands Jesus Christ as well as Rev. Moon. . . . There isn't anyone who has the same author-ity to speak as Rev. Moon."[1] And that includes the Bible.

Purpose of Creation/   The specific teaching of the *Divine Principle* can best be divided into three areas: the first Adam, the second Adam and the Lord of the Second Advent. The first Adam and Eve were God's initial human creations who fell into sin. The second Adam was Jesus Christ who died on the cross because of the faithlessness of the Jews. The Lord of the Second Advent is the Messiah who must come to establish the Kingdom of Heaven here on earth. These three Adams comprise God's plan for fulfilling the original goals of creation.

In order to understand the message of the *Divine Principle*, readers must grasp the fundamental theme which underlies all of its basic concepts: Whether positive or negative (DP 21), ex-ternal or internal (DP 21), Yang or Yin (DP 26), all concepts are divided into dualities of which male and female is the thread that sews them all together. Creation itself is understood after this pattern, for God, prior to creating the universe, existed as "the internal masculine subject." In making the universe, he created an "external feminine object" (DP 25). God as subject gives love as an emotional force to the object; creation as object returns beauty as an emotional force to the subject. This interaction brings perfect joy to the subject, and thus the relationship between God and creation is fulfilled.

Moreover, just as God himself has both male and female qualities, all of his creation likewise can be divided into male and female elements. A plant has its stamen and pistil. Animals are either male or female. Mankind also is composed of men and women. That is why marriage is essential for a full knowledge of God, so that the unification of a man and a woman in a marriage can correspond with God who possesses both qualities.

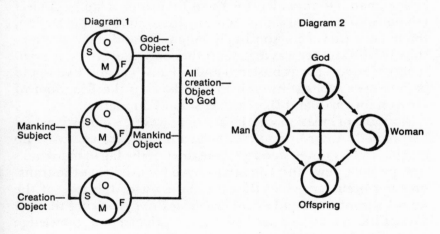

Nevertheless, God always maintains a subject-position over mankind and creation, as can be seen in Diagram 1. Creation, meanwhile, always exists as an object of God and mankind. And mankind is both an object of God and a subject over creation.

The ultimate purpose of creation is expressed in the concept of the Four Position Foundation, which depicts how God relates to mankind and all creation. As is shown in Diagram 2 God at the top center forms the subject-position, which is the base for all God-centered foundations. Man and woman were originally created to mature and marry forming the object-positions, while also creating a third object-position through their offspring. In this ideal state all points would then engage in reciprocal relationships of subject and object-positions.

Diagrams 1 and 2 (as well as 3 and 4 on page 77) are taken from the *Divine Principle and Its Application* and the *120-Day Training Manual*. Diagrams such as these are extensively employed by the Unification Church to train its members to become leaders.

The Fall of Man/   God's highest expression of the duality of male and female was his creation of Adam and Eve, the first man and woman. He intended for them to assume a subject/object relationship with himself in their growth to spiritual perfection, for initially they were spiritually immature and their relationship with each other was that of brother and sister. In their eventual perfected state as husband and wife, Adam and Eve would be able to establish through their offspring the Kingdom of Heaven on earth and the Four Position Foundation.

The goal of creation was thwarted, however, when Adam and Eve sinned. According to the *Divine Principle*, for centuries no one has rightly understood the true story of the fall of mankind's first parents. Jews and Christians have believed that the transgression occurred when they ate the fruit of the tree of the knowledge of good and evil. The *Divine Principle* claims that the tree of life symbolizes perfected Adam, the tree of knowledge symbolizes Eve and the fall came through Eve's illicit love affairs.

The *Divine Principle* explains the sexual nature of the fall as follows: Prior to the fall, Adam and Eve were naked and were not ashamed; after the fall they were ashamed of their nakedness and so they sewed fig leaves into aprons to cover their lower parts. This indicates that sexuality was involved in the fall, for, as the *Divine Principle* states, "It is the nature of man to conceal an area of transgression. They covered their sexual parts, clearly indicating that they were ashamed of the sexual areas of their bodies because they had committed sin through them"(DP 72).

When man was created, Lucifer became extremely envious of God's love for man, since God loved Adam and Eve as his children and Lucifer as his servant. Lucifer also saw Eve's great beauty and desired her sexually. At this time Lucifer had not fallen himself, but because of jealousy and lust he entered into an unlawful relationship with Eve. The sexual intercourse between a spirit being and a human being constituted not only Lucifer's fall but the *spiritual* fall of man.

While Eve participated in her illicit relationship with Lucifer, she received spiritual insight and realized that she had violated the purpose of creation. She knew then that her intended spouse was not Lucifer but Adam. Subsequently she had intercourse with Adam in an attempt to restore her position with God. Adam, however was still spiritually immature. Consequently they entered into a relationship which constituted the *physical* fall of man.

Thus there is a dual aspect to the fall: a *spiritual* fall and a *physical* fall, both of which have to do with their sexuality. Diagrams 3 and 4 are used to depict this state of affairs.

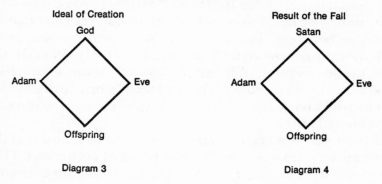

Diagram 3   Diagram 4

The Second Adam/   The fall of man presented a problem for

God, for by it God's plans were thwarted. Since the fall, it has been God's will to restore men to himself through *spiritual* and *physical* redemption. People in every age from Abel to Noah to Abraham have failed to obey God. Finally, however, there lived an obedient man. His name was Jesus.

The *Divine Principle* states that about four hundred years in advance of Jesus, God sent Malachi to the Jewish nation to prepare them for the coming of the Messiah (DP 423). Meanwhile, God had Gautama Buddha and Confucius prepare the Asian world and Socrates the Hellenist world for the coming of the Messiah. All religions and cultures were to unify under the acceptance of Jesus. But God's will was tragically thwarted by the crucifixion.

The reason for Jesus' crucifixion can now be revealed. The major cause keeping people from believing in Jesus was John the Baptist's failure to serve and minister to Jesus. Despite the fact that Jesus identified John as Elijah, John denied it. Since John had more influence with the Jews than Jesus did, he made Jesus sound like an imposter. That is why Jesus said of John in Luke 7: 28, "I tell you, among those born of women none is greater than John; yet he who is least in the kingdom of God is greater than he." God had intended for John to be the greatest prophet, but because of his disbelief he is the least in God's kingdom.

It should be noted that the *Divine Principle* does not claim that Jesus sinned or failed to obey God. Rather, in realizing that he would not be accepted as the Messiah by the Jewish nation, Jesus took the only course available to him. He "resolved to take the cross as the condition of indemnity to pay for the accomplishment of even the spiritual salvation of man" when he discovered that he could not accomplish both the spiritual and the physical salvation (DP 151).

If Jesus had not been crucified, he would have married the perfect mate, who was to be from the house of Zechariah.[2] Thus He would have established God's perfect family on earth, accomplishing both the spiritual and the physical salvation of man. As it was, however, "his body was invaded by Satan, and he was killed. . . . In this manner, however devout a man of faith may be, he cannot fulfill physical salvation by redemption through Jesus' crucifixion alone" (DP 147-48).

Moreover, according to the *Divine Principle*, Jesus did not appear in bodily form after his physical death and prior to his ascension. Rather, he was "a being transcendent of time and space" (DP 360) and appeared to his disciples as a spirit being. Thus the book argues against the physical resurrection of Jesus.

It is obvious that this understanding of Jesus and God raises questions concerning the traditional notion of the Trinity. The *Divine Principle* essentially rejects this doctrine, reasoning, for example, that when in the Bible God speaks in the plural he is not speaking from the standpoint of a "trinity" but as the head over the angels (DP 76). Jesus, who took an active part in the creation of the universe according to traditional understanding of passages such as John 1:1-3, is seen by this book as taking part in creation only in the sense that all perfected men do so because they fulfill the purpose of creation (DP 211).

Furthermore, the Spirit of God, which was instrumental in Mary's conception of Jesus, was not the Holy Spirit but the same Spirit which helped to conceive "Isaac, Samson, Samuel, Elijah, and John the Baptist."[3] This doctrine further erodes the belief that Jesus was God prior to his physical birth.

Finally, the doctrine of spiritual salvation is put in terms of the duality of male and female. Since Jesus is the male element, "there must be a True Mother with a True Father, in order to give rebirth to fallen children as children of goodness. She is the Holy Spirit" (DP 215). God the Father, Jesus and the Holy Spirit do form a trinity in the *Divine Principle*, but not as God in three Persons. Rather they establish a spiritual foundation for salvation. After the Lord of the Second Advent comes, "all mankind will be restored to God by forming trinities with Him."[4]

The divinity of Jesus, therefore, is limited to his being a "perfected man." Since perfected men may be said "to even possess deity," Jesus "may well be called God. Nevertheless, he can by no means be God himself " (DP 210-11). While he was on earth,

Jesus was no different from any other person, "except for the fact that he was without original sin" (DP 212). In summation, Jesus saved man spiritually but not physically because he was crucified by the Jews and the Romans. Therefore, Jesus was unable to meet his perfect mate and establish the Kingdom of Heaven on earth. And thus the Messiah or Lord of the Second Advent must come to complete God's purpose for creation.

The Lord of the Second Advent/   It is necessary here to emphasize that the purpose of creation to perfect man spiritually requires that the process be accomplished only through physical life on earth. There is essentially no difference between a Christian, regardless of how devout he may be, and an Old Testament saint; neither have been able to clear themselves of original sin or "remove themselves from the lineage of Satan." The Lord of the Second Advent "must be born on earth, in flesh," in order to accomplish man's physical salvation (DP 368-69).

The *Divine Principle* devotes a major portion of its study to numerology. The number 2,000 provides the key to the coming of the Lord of the Second Advent. The *Divine Principle* states that Jesus came 2,000 years after Abraham, during which time God had prepared the first coming of the Messiah (DP 499). Therefore, the Lord of the Second Advent will come 2,000 years after Jesus, during which time God has prepared the second coming of the Messiah. It may be concluded from this that the Messiah is coming at any moment, if he has not already arrived.

The *Divine Principle* not only dates the Second Advent but indicates the birthplace as well. Basing its case on Revelation 7: 2-4 ("Then I saw another angel ascend from the rising of the sun, with the seal of the living God"), the book concludes that Christ will be born in a country in the east. This, it continues, has meant "from ancient times" the nations of Korea, Japan and China (DP 519-20).

The *Divine Principle* examines each of the three countries as possibilities for the birthplace. It notes that Japan is a nation

which has worshiped Amaterasuomikami and has entered the
period of the Second Advent as a totalitarian nation which has
persecuted Christians in Korea. China as a communist nation is
on the Satanic side. The *Divine Principle*, therefore, concludes
that the Lord of the Second Advent will be born in Korea (DP
520).

People will be able to determine who the Lord of the Second
Advent is by whether he has subjugated Satan absolutely and has
provided the pattern by which each person can subjugate Satan
completely. The Messiah must discover Satan's hidden crime,
which was his seduction of Eve, in order to subjugate him. He
must also re-establish the subject/object relationship with God
through the Four Position Foundation.

It might be assumed at this point that the *Divine Principle*
proclaims Sun Myung Moon as the Lord of the Second Advent.
It does not. Neither the *Divine Principle* nor Moon himself will
declare publicly today that he is the Messiah. There are a good
many reasons for this, but proselytizing is the strongest. Moon's
followers believe that potential converts will react negatively
to their doctrine of the second coming, if presented at initial
confrontations. They further believe that those who hear and
reject the revelations imparted to Moon by God will be condemned. Therefore, their desire and effort is to gather the lost
under their loving wings and then introduce the doctrine of the
Divine Principle. Each convert will then decide within his own
heart who the Lord of the Second Advent is. Of course, their
hearts are quickly molded to regard Moon as Master and True
Father.

People of all faiths would have accepted Jesus as the Messiah
save for his death. The Lord of the Second Advent now assumes
Jesus' role and all religions will unite under him. In fact, everyone who is conscientious will come to accept the Lord of the Second Advent (DP 189-90): "In the Completed Testament Age
people will be justified not by observing the Mosaic Law or believing in Jesus, but by following and attending the Lord of the
new world."[6]

Moon's Warning to Christians/   Although inviting to people of
other faiths and beliefs, the *Divine Principle* concludes with an
ominous warning to Christians. It claims that Christians today
will be like the priests and rabbis of Jesus' day, the "first to persecute the Messiah" (DP 533). Christians will cling to their archaic
beliefs and will be blind to the truths of the new age. The warning is ominous: "Innumerable Christians of today are dashing
on the way which they think will lead them to the Kingdom of
Heaven. Nevertheless, this road is apt to lead them into hell"
(DP 535). Christians must accept the revelations within the *Divine Principle* and the Lord of the Second Advent or be damned.

THE INNER TEACHINGS

7

THE PROCESS OF INDOCTRINATION WITHIN the Unification Church is a well-designed system to take adherents from simple, universal doctrines of the church to the esoteric teachings of Sun Myung Moon. The inner teachings of this movement are only revealed to those followers who have accepted the basic tenets of the *Divine Principle*. Nevertheless, as the mass media has spotlighted Moon more and more, so the inner teachings are gradually being disclosed to the general public.

The Esoteric Documents/ The esoteric documents which dictate the conditioned thoughts of the followers of Rev. Moon are the *Master Speaks*, the *Divine Principle and Its Application*, the *120-Day Training Manual* and the *New Hope News* newsletters. Many other works also supplement Moon's teachings (for example, *Unification Thought* and *Unification Theology and Christian Thought*), but they are rather like textbooks which provide further details and explanations for already accepted tenets. The other four, however, go beyond the scope of the *Divine Principle* in one important way; they formulate arguments that Rev. Moon is the Messiah, a belief only meant for adherents of his movement.

The *Master Speaks* is the most famous work of the four. If it is not more known than the *Divine Principle* to the news media, it is, at least, more sought after and used by them. The reason for this is that the *Master Speaks* is a collection of talks which Moon has personally given. Although they are translations of Moon's words and consequently often translated in the third person, the critical quotes are in the first person ("I am your brain," for example).[1] Furthermore, statements which unabashedly exude Moon's political ambitions and messianic egoism are mostly found in this document.

The *Master Speaks* is circulated at all of the centers of the Unification Church and is incessantly perused by its members. The talks are voluminous and terribly redundant so that the constant strain of concentrating on it may be enough to help regiment a mind to a state of passivity and to indoctrinate the reader into the unswerving belief that Moon is the Lord of the Second Advent. Others who are uncommitted to Moon will probably be bored to death with it. But for the follower of Moon, the *Master Speaks* is effective in eliciting the correct thoughts and emotions needed to mold a productive worker for the movement.

The *Divine Principle and Its Application* was a document more important in the earlier years of the church in this country and prior to Moon's tours here. It existed as the teaching instrument of the church for twelve years until the *Divine Principle* could be translated and published in English in its expanded form in 1973. It also served as a study guide at the training centers in the sixties. While it is systematic and clear in its style, it also stays close in subject matter to its mother work.

Young Oon Kim is the author of the *Divine Principle and Its Application*. She was born on March 27, 1915, became an early convert to Moon's movement, and was Moon's first missionary to the United States in January of 1959. Her book is important because it presents the best insight into Moon's doctrine on the spirit world and his alliance with spirit beings.

The most explicit work of the four is the *120-Day Training Manual*, which is taught by various church leaders (especially Ken Sudo) primarily at the Barrytown seminary in New York. It has replaced Kim's book as the study guide of the church and has been more effective in instructing potential leaders of the church. Although, like the *Master Speaks*, it is a compilation of talks, the presentations are personal and practical; individual experiences are closely related to the *Divine Principle*. Thus the manual contains many unabashed statements which are reserved for a select few.

Finally the *New Hope News* newsletters offer scattered information which is taught in the church but is not in written form elsewhere. Such accounts as Moon's dialogue with Lucifer in their spiritual battle provide insight into Moon's character and his followers' reverence for him. It also presents the church's attitude toward its critics, the progress of its growth both in terms of people and real estate, a detailed history of the church, the activities of its front organizations and, quite simply, its propaganda among the followers.

These documents constitute the inner teachings of Moon and his church. They define the failure of Jesus, declare Moon to be the Messiah, outline the path of indemnity and discuss the activity of the spirit world. More significant is the presence of a spiritual power which underlies the dogma that they teach. For that reason each point should be read with that in mind.

Jesus, the Failure/ Rev. Moon defines Jesus as a failure. Although the people of Israel are to blame for his death, Moon has no reserve in saying that Jesus was like all the other holy men who failed. "Abraham was the father of faith, Moses was a man of faith, Jesus was the son of man, trying to carry out his mission at the cost of his life. But they are, in a way, failures."[2]

Jesus was selected to be the Lord of lords, but since he could not complete his mission he did not attain that position. After John the Baptist had failed him, it was clear that the Jews would not follow him. Consequently God informed Jesus of his coming crucifixion through Moses and Elijah at his transfiguration. The fact that Jesus had to die grieved God's heart. "God was not happy at all to see the resurrected Jesus,"[3] for Moon emphasizes that, when Jesus was crucified on the cross, "God and Jesus lost everything."[4]

Nevertheless, Moon says that members of the Unification Church are "in a position to save and liberate Jesus Christ and end his anguish," for they are "the only people who truly understand the heart of Jesus, the anguish of Jesus, and the hope of Jesus."[5] Furthermore, "it is a wonderful fact that while Jesus did not have anyone left behind him who could inherit what was accomplished by him,we have our descendents, our group, who are going to inherit what we accomplished while in life even if we may have to die here."[6]

It is obvious that Moon's great cause is not preaching salvation through the death and resurrection of Jesus but establishing the kingdom of God on earth. Moon, therefore, claims his mission is greater than Jesus'. In the *Master Speaks*, Moon frequently compares Jesus with himself, his movement and followers. He says, "You can compare yourself with Jesus Christ, and feel you can be greater than Jesus himself."[7] He tells his followers that they must be greater and better than Jesus and that they must accomplish more than Jesus did. Moon reasons that, because Jesus could only gather twelve disciples while alive and Moon has gathered far more, his group is greater. Furthermore, Jesus had only gathered locally while Moon has gathered worldwide. Moon says, "No heroes in the past, no saints or holy men in the past, like Jesus, or Confucius, have excelled us."[8]

With so much emphasis on the insignificance of Jesus' life, it is only natural for a follower to ask Moon (as one did), "Well— most of us have come from Christian backgrounds—and a question that has really been bothering me is exactly how much did Jesus accomplish, because it seems like he accomplished very little. I just wondered how much he really did accomplish."

Moon's reply: "Nothing. There was but one thing left. He

died for God and heaven—that is the only thing he accomplished. He died, 'Not my will, but I'll die for God'—that is the
only thing he left. Nothing was accomplished, nobody, no disciples at all, nothing, just death. Christianity started after his
death anyway."[9]

Moon the Successor/   A close examination of materials distributed by the Unification Church reveals an interesting use of pronouns referring to Christ and Moon. Although not totally con-
sistent, pronouns which refer to Jesus are written in small letters such as "he." This may be worth little notice since even some
Bibles do the same, but what makes it deserve attention is that
pronouns referring to Moon and his wife are written in capital
letters such as "He" and "She."

The fact is that Moon's followers do believe he is the Messiah,
and the inner teachings support this belief. While spoken of as
Father, Master or True Parent, he is always assumed to be the
Messiah. Others outside of the church, his followers say, will in-
evitably believe as well, for, as his movement sweeps across
America, "then they can understand that Rev. Moon is the Mes-
siah, the Lord of the Second Advent."[10] Or, if they study the
Divine Principle and particularly "if only they can understand the
fall of man they can understand that Father is the Messiah."[11]
Furthermore, "Father is visible God."[12]

Although a messiah, Moon is still viewed as a man, albeit a perfected man, within his theology; as such he will die and pass to
the Heavenly Kingdom. Consequently, he has been given a time
limit to fulfill certain, ascribed steps if he is to succeed in establishing the Kingdom of Heaven on earth. The four successive
conditions are the perfection of the individual, family, nation
and world. Moon has completed the first three and is now in the
process of fulfilling the fourth, after which he can pass to the
spirit world confident that his followers will continue his mission.

Meanwhile, the relationship between the True Parents and
the Unified Family is that of parents with their sons and daugh-

ters, but the relationship between Jesus and Christians is that between the Son of God and his servants. Moon himself won the sonship and was blessed by God in 1960. He now has the authority on earth by God to forgive sins. There is no sin which he cannot forgive, because he has sacrificed his life by shedding blood when he fought with Satan. Therefore, if Moon says that your sins are forgiven, his will is approved by God. Moon himself is sinless.

All power comes through the True Parents. A follower must become "a crazy man, crazy woman, just wanting to see the True Parents."[13] Furthermore, Moon says, "If you call me your True Parents, you must assume the image and the likeness of me,"[14] a statement echoing Paul's reference to Christ in Romans 8. Another Christian principle which Moon twists for his own ends is sacrificing one's own life. "There will be Master's disciples to be crucified and you are going to be willing to die in place of him."[15]

Moon's job is to comfort God's heart. Therefore, he must set a better standard than any human being in history, including Jesus Christ. "During my first 3 years of public ministry, just as Jesus did, I had to go through severe hardships culminating in the torture of prison life, which was more for me than Jesus' cross."[16] Furthermore, "I had to accomplish all left unaccomplished by my predecessor. . . . When you think of that, you must feel indebted to me and you cannot lift your face before me."[17]

Rev. Moon has endured great hardship and suffered much pain for his mission. Even now he is still going through a difficult path. For example, he must watch and study TV and English until three o'clock in the morning. If anyone is entitled to complain, he says, he is the first, but he doesn't because he wants to be an example to his followers. Since he had to fight the vast spirit world, subjugating Satan, "If there be any God, I think that He has got to love me. If God does not love me, then there is no God—that is my thought."[18]

Indemnity or the Work's Trip/   Indemnity is the primary doctrine within Moon's theology which enslaves his followers into serving him body and soul. In one stroke it strips away God's grace in Christ and institutes a standard of salvation by works. Young Oon Kim states that the Hindus and Buddhists call it the law of karma. She describes it as paying God back a little of what is owed, which God accepts and thus forgives the balance. Christians are wrong to believe that Jesus canceled the law of indemnity, she says. Individuals themselves have to pay for their own restitution of sin either in the flesh or spirit.

There are several methods of paying these debts. One quick method is fasting. Fasting has been widely practiced among various religious people, but the reason has not been clear. "Now we know," says Kim, "that their fasting is payment to Satan for release."[19] That is why there is so much emphasis placed on fasting within the Unification Church.

Other methods are fundraising and recruiting. Within these two methods Moon stimulates intense competition among his followers. He frequently exhorts Americans to excel beyond their foreign counterparts, particularly the Japanese. He also warns whites that if they don't achieve his set goals he will replace them with blacks and yellows. Furthermore, Unification brothers must surpass their sisters' performance if they are to maintain their spiritual position. Moon admonishes his followers, "When you live in the church, if you don't witness to the people, and restore the material for the church you are parasites; if you don't bring in spiritual children and want to get blessed in marriage, you are thieves."[20]

There is further pressure in that the entire world, the universe and the spirit world is depending on them as a group to satisfy each level of indemnity. And, if they fail at one level, all that has been done before will become nothing. The same holds true for the individual. He may work for years and succeed to a high level, but if he should fail or turn away before becoming perfect, all is lost.

To enter the Kingdom of God, a person must be perfect, for perfected men have no need for forgiveness. Descendents of

perfected parents will be born free from original sin, and therefore will have no need for a savior. The man of perfection is one
who has achieved the unity of the spiritual side and fleshly side
of satisfying the law of indemnity.

In the past God gave help to men, but now people are on their
own. There is no need for help from heaven. Genuine good
sons and daughters recover everything believing in God, without his help. "This follows the principle that man's perfection
must be accomplished finally by his own effort without God's
help, and also to indemnify man's past failures."[21]

The Spirit World/   According to Moon, in the beginning God
created the cosmos composed of two separate worlds, the physical world and the spiritual world. Man himself is a physical being
and a spiritual being and is therefore the mediator between the
physical world and the spiritual world. Only man can connect
the two worlds. God cannot because "God, the Creator, is infinite, invisible Spirit and does not appear fully in any finite or
visible form."[22]

Once man had direct dominion over the physical world; and
God had indirect dominion over the physical world through
man. Man, however, relinquished his authority to Satan when
Adam and Eve fell. Although Satan was expelled from the spirit
world and has no power in the spiritual realm, he has established
his power on earth in the form of materialism and communism.
Thus, God has fought Satan to regain earth for man and has
been on the defensive until Moon was able to subjugate Satan.
Now the satanic power is doomed to decline, and by the year
1980 the satanic sovereignty will have fallen.

Spirit-men are beings who have separated from their physical
bodies and live forever in the spirit world. They, like all things,
must progress through three stages: Formation, Growth and
Perfection. A spirit-man in the Formation Stage is known as a
Form-Spirit; in the Growth Stage, as a Life-Spirit; and in the
Perfection Stage, as a Divine-Spirit. During the Old Testament
age men who obeyed the law and walked with God became

Form-Spirits. After Jesus ushered in the New Testament age, those who believed in him became Life-Spirits. These Life-Spirits inhabit paradise where Jesus dwells. A spirit-man at the Divine-Spirit level is one with God and radiates a bright luminescence. Their dwelling place is called heaven. Ultimately all men are destined to become Divine-Spirits and dwell in the spiritual heaven, while hell is the realm inhabited by spirits who have not yet grown to the Form-Spirit level. Until the Completed Testament age the spiritual heaven has been vacant because no one had become a Divine-Spirit before proceeding into the spirit world, but now Moon has paved the path for all.

A spirit-man can progress only in conjunction with his physical body. Once he dies, therefore, he cannot progress. Consequently, spirit-men who die before reaching Perfection must descend to earth in order to complete their resurrection through the medium of earthly people. Those in the spirit world must depend upon the people on earth for their complete resurrection. (This is similar to the concept of indulgences in late medieval Catholicism and the Bodhisattvas in Buddhism in which one man's merits can surpass the requirements for his own salvation to the extent that the surplus saves one or more others.) Thus the spirit-beings will cooperate and aid earthly people. At this time, not only good spirits, but "evil spirits are descending. If their influence contributes to the indemnity for the new dispensation, they also benefit."[23]

All spirit beings are ministering to Moon and are anxious to follow him wherever he goes because they know that he is the Lord of the Second Advent, the Avatar of the New Age. There were divisions among the spirit-men, such as Christians against Buddhists, but now they are all one behind Moon. Kim says that spirit-beings such as the Mother Mary, Buddha and Confucius are directing people to the Unification Church. People will begin to follow Moon if they listen to the spirit world.

After encountering Jesus, Moon's spiritual senses were fully opened, enabling him to communicate with the spirit world. Moon can call for and talk to Moses or Abraham or anyone else.

None knew why they had failed until Moon told them. Moon's most devoted followers can also converse with Jesus and the others. Through their spiritual senses they can perceive the spirit world and develop such abilities as clairvoyance and clairaudience.

In the spirit world spirit beings breathe love just as in the physical world people breathe air. So also, if people in the Family elevate to a certain standard of love, they will be able to communicate with the spirit world. Furthermore, if they love Moon enough, they will be able to see him face to face in daily life. It is a precious experience to see Moon in a vision or dream or feel one with him. Followers are told to recall and make statistics. "If you go on cultivating such experiences, you will reach the point where your heart will be broadened to be a channel of communication with the spirit world."[24]

Spiritual Power/ "Mr. Moon in deep meditation can project himself and be seen just as Jesus has been able to project himself and be seen by the saints. This is one of the marks of the messiahs,"[25] stated Fletcher, the spirit who speaks through Arthur Ford, the infamous medium. At a sitting on November 2, 1964, without Moon and at a sitting on March 18, 1965, with Moon, Fletcher confirmed the Spirit of Truth's use of Moon as an instrument through whom it is able to speak.

Mediums and seers like Ford and Jeane Dixon, who said, "Bless you, Reverend Moon, for your message,"[26] have lauded Moon and his movement. They feel that he is a highly sensitized person who has been sent by the Creative Mind, called God by some, to be a teacher and a revealer. Meanwhile leaders in the Unification Church have used these affirmations for public relations. While relatively unknown in the West in the sixties, Moon was particularly aided by Ford in having his name appear before the public.

Nevertheless, Moon and his followers were quite disappointed with the sittings with Ford because Fletcher did not recognize Moon to be the one and only Messiah: "But Mr. Moon is just one in a long line of people who have been used as revelators—he is not the last—he is not the first—but in this hour, he is being used in a great way."[27] Moon holds that spirits are dependent on man. Apparently Moon and his lieutenants did not realize that within the occult man is dependent on the spirits and no man receives all the glory.

In spite of this drawback, Moon has used these sittings as evidence that the spirit world recognizes him as a Messiah. Furthermore, Moon says that everyone in the spirit world is on his side and that he and his people are going to be in control of the spirit world. Since Moon cannot personally reach everyone, the spirit world will help him move the hearts of people, a phenomenon which will occur more frequently.

In the war between God and Satan, Moon sees satanic power mobilizing the Christian churches to attack him and the Unification Church. Billions of spirit-men, including ancestors, however, will descend and help Moon fulfill God's will: "Those who are against our movement and persecute us will be punished by the spirit side," says Moon.[28]

Comforted with the belief that all the spirit world is behind him, it is only natural for Moon to believe that he is invincible. This same belief he encourages among his followers, telling them that they will resemble him and have power with untold energy. "If all of you are united into a fist like this, I will be the one who will use the fist," he says. "Then whatever thing the fist meets will be broken down."[29]

IV

**"JESUS SAID TO HIM,
'I AM THE WAY AND THE TRUTH,
AND THE LIFE;
NO ONE COMES TO THE FATHER,
BUT BY ME.' "**

(JOHN 14:6)

A CHRISTIAN RESPONSE

8

THE WAY OF JESUS IS THE WAY of love. He demonstrated his love for us by laying down his life that we might have the way to God the Father. And so as Christians we daily walk with him, learning to receive the love he has for us and learning to share it with those in the world so that the touch of God's love might produce in them a desire to follow the way of Jesus. In Jesus is love, and in Jesus alone is the way to walk in love.

A Loving Witness/ There is no best method to share Christ with members of the Unification Church. The Spirit will discern for you what attitude, demeanor and scriptural line to follow for the particular individual you might meet. But no amount of good intentions and good will will make up for a strong faith in Christ and a solid biblical understanding of Christ as Savior, Lord and God. Your personal relationship with Christ, however, may itself be the best testimony.

A personal relationship with Christ is like a beacon in the night; it gives sight to what needs to be seen, it offers direction and it relieves the fear of the dark. So a Christian becomes a beacon in the darkness of the Moon cult. The power of the Lord in our lives, our faith and belief in him and his love abiding in us: If anything can touch the hearts of members of the Unification Church, certainly these qualities will be the most lasting. If they see in our lives victory over sin because of the power of the Lord, perhaps then they will see that neither they nor Moon can overcome the sins in their lives but that only Christ can free them. If they see our faith in Jesus as the Savior who has died and conquered death for our total salvation, as the Lord who rules our lives completely and as the God who has authority over all, perhaps then they will see that the only meaningful direction in life is not being a slave of one in quest for power and wealth but being led with integrity by Christ. If they see the love which flows between Jesus and us, perhaps then they will see that a love pure and sensitive is not one wrought with the fears and guilt implicit in Moon's movement but is in Jesus who says, "Come to me, all who labor and are heavy laden, and I will give you rest" (Matthew 11:28).

In sharing your faith with followers of any cult it is essential to love them in Christ. If we encounter them as enemies on a battlefield, if we pit our beliefs against their beliefs, if with our desire to be right we overrule the Spirit's love for them as lost children, then whether or not we win or lose the battle, we lose the war. And worse: They will lose all. Thus, we must humble ourselves to Christ's love and let it flow through us.

Nevertheless, only to love and not to stand on the truth is to water down the saving power of the gospel. Love is necessary, but so is truth. Now truth is unlike the desire to be right. Truth humbly walks with the Lord, not in front of him. In fact, Christ himself is the truth. If we are to know the truth, we must know Christ. If we are to have the truth, we must have Christ; we must experience him in our lives as Savior, Lord and God.

If we are deficient in our knowledge and commitment to Christ when we witness, we will either lose our nerve, be unable to speak with power, or worse yet, come away not knowing what happened. If we are not deficient in knowledge and commitment, the same results may occur. It is not enough to have love and truth. One more thing is necessary.

We must be led by Christ's Spirit. Our witnessing must be in God's will. In God's own wisdom is the timing just right for planting, sowing and reaping the Word. Our task might be all or any or none. Only the Spirit knows. Thus, we must prayerfully allow the Spirit to guide us into and through our encounters, for the power of salvation is in him and not in us.

Since it is God's power, however, any believer at whatever stage in his walk with the Lord can be a usable instrument of God. It does not require time and maturity to share Christ. A newborn believer may be more effective than a veteran evangelist of many years. You neither have to have a particular desire nor experience to be suitable for witnessing to members of the Unified Family. It is neither necessary to have a mission-like desire to share Christ with them, nor do you have to have had past experience within the Unification Church. I have had neither, but the Lord has called me out for this task. It is enough to say that the Lord directs, and to him goes all the glory.

Nonetheless, the Lord does not ask us to be mechanical or blind when he uses us. We must have love and truth; for love will help us to discern their needs and truth will answer them. As a matter of fact, it is a sure sign you are not led by his Spirit, if you lack God's love and his truth.

The Question of Deprogramming/　　Many people believe that deprogramming is the only option in rescuing their children or friends from the Unification Church; others believe that deprogramming is ethically and legally wrong. It may be easy for a person untouched by that problem to make a judgment, but for those who are faced with that situation it is agonizing to abide by the law at the sacrifice of their loved ones. Deprogramming, therefore, becomes a tough question, one not easily answered or dismissed without a hard look at the teaching of our Lord and Savior, Jesus Christ.

The extreme difficulty which parents have in their dialogues with their children is what drives many of them to employ kidnapping and deprogramming. Their children are either so indoctrinated into Moon's teachings that they can converse in circles for hours or so vulnerable to family influences that they resist any personal contact with the outside world. Those who are well disciplined into the *Divine Principle* can quote Scriptures right and left to support every belief they have, or they can interpret any Bible verse which you can quote and twist it into their line of belief. Thus, it is frustrating to try to debate theology or philosophy with them. Those who are weak in their belief avoid any conversations which might test their faith. Either they will allow a stronger Family member to control them if they must encounter their folks or friends, or they will flee if they are approached on the streets by witnessing Christians, or they will close their ears and sing loudly if they are forced to confront an opposing belief. These difficulties are enough to force many parents to attempt deprogramming as an alternate method of rescue.

Deprogramming, however, is not the answer according to various psychologists, law officials and Christians. Some psychologists say that deprogramming is simply a reverse pattern of brainwashing.[1] The Unification Church may be brainwashing its converts, but whether they are or not, deprogramming cannot be condoned, for although the content is different, the method is the same. Thus, if one is wrong, so is the other.

Police officers and judges usually see no legal justification in parents' kidnapping and deprogramming their son or daughter if the person is an adult. In a society where each individual has the right to live whatever life he or she chooses within the laws of the land, the standard of happiness is relative to the individual himself. Therefore, the courts strongly defend the freedom of religion.

Many Christians contend that "if it is permissible to deprogram a disciple of Sun Myung Moon, then why not also a 'Jew for Jesus' or a fundamentalist?"[2] In other words, if deprogramming is left to the discretion of the deprogrammer, who will be safe to believe in what they believe?

But are these reasons not to deprogram good enough? When the government hesitates to deal with Moon and his church because of its fear of violating the separation of state and religion, when law officials and the court are less than enthusiastic about investigating the operations of the movement because there are so many movements like it, when the Christian church finds passivity more desirable than spiritual warfare, then what choice do parents have other than deprogramming? People can present a nice, simple analysis of the problem, but an analysis won't solve the problem. Deprogramming may not be laudable, but at least sometimes it works.

For a Christian, however, whether it "works" cannot be the final standard. There are many things in this world that "work" in the sense that they will produce a certain result; both aspirin and heroin will get rid of a headache. The point is that Moon's indoctrination works in the first place because it fills a void in a member's life. If this underlying, personal need is not recognized or dealt with, even the most technically "effective" deprogramming will be ultimately useless. Thus a stranger to Christ may be able to deprogram one of Moon's followers, but he cannot fill the void which has been created. If a person's hunger for reality is not met by the True and Living God, it will only feed on idols, whether they be Moon's doctrines or materialism or something else.

Is a person in the Unification Church pursuing his own desires any worse off than a person in the world pursuing his own desires? Many people in the Unification Church are happy, content and fulfilled. Will they be any happier in the world? Many converts would have less reason to live outside of the church than within it. Whether a person is conformed to Moon's desires or to his parents' desires makes no difference, for the ultimate meaning of life is in the crucified Savior and being conformed to his desires.

In the final analysis, the goal of life is not "happiness" or any other emotional state, but reconciliation with God, which is accomplished only by being born again in Christ. Worldly happiness is temporal, but life in Christ is joy eternal. Therefore, a Christian must share Christ with those in the Unification Church. Our primary goal must be to bring the person to Christ, not to take him away from the Unification Church.

If a person accepts the fullness of the Lord, then he will be ready to accept Christ's teachings and reject Moon's, but acceptance must be the first consideration. Jesus himself says, "For God so loved the world that he gave his only Son, that whoever believes in him should not perish but have eternal life" (John 3:16).

A Christian must respect the right of another person to accept Christ or reject him, for God has given this right to everyone. When he was questioned by a certain young ruler about obtaining eternal life, Jesus said that he must follow him (Luke 18:18-22), but he did not coerce him. Throughout his ministry on earth, Jesus always allowed the individual to choose to follow him; and whenever any follower desired to leave, Jesus never stood in his way. Clearly this sets apart Jesus' conduct from Moon's effort to maintain the loyalty of his followers *and also* sets apart Jesus' respect for others' beliefs from kidnapping and deprogramming, which are, in themselves, methods of determinism.

After all, God is all powerful and he will open the door to those who sincerely seek him. "There is none like thee, O LORD; thou art great, and thy name is great in might" (Jeremiah 10:6). The question, therefore, is not: "Is deprogramming right or wrong?" but "Does God have power over all?" The believer will certainly answer, "Yes." The unbeliever will respond, "I believe in no Lord. Therefore, the question has no validity," in which case deprogramming needs no justification. The believer, however, must discern matters more deeply.

One of the most basic of all theological contrasts is that which the Bible sets up between the grace of God and the works of man: "By grace you have been saved through faith; and this is not your own doing, it is the gift of God—not because of works, lest any man should boast" (Ephesians 2:8-9). Man's activity has a place in the scheme of God's grace, but the function of human effort (in witnessing, for example) is to present the *opportunity* for an occasion of grace, not to contrive the occasion itself. Deprogramming, on the other hand, is an attempt to take the act of grace into human hands, to manipulate the mechanics of grace to a predetermined result. It is certainly true that deprogramming has opened the way for some to become Christians. This does not imply, however, a Christian endorsement of human efforts to construct an occasion of grace; it simply means that deprogramming, like anything else, can *become* an occasion of grace by the sovereignty of God.

A Christian must share Jesus as Christ in all situations but not be a party to anything which is dishonest. If the follower of Moon is well versed in Scripture, a Christian must concentrate on the Bible's affirmation of Christ as Savior, Lord and God, and not join in lengthy and useless discussions on fine points of doctrine. If a member of the Unified Family has been trained to fear opposing views, a Christian must be patient, sensitive and gentle, and not allow frustration or desperation to interfere with the work of God's Spirit. Above all, a Christian must trust the Lord, because "he who is in you is greater than he who is in the world" (1 John 4:4) and "the Lord is not slow about his promise as some count slowness, but is forbearing toward you, not wishing that any should perish but that all should reach repentance" (2 Peter 3:9).

Judgment on the Christian Church/   Several months ago I heard a Christian minister on the radio exhort Christians not to pass judgment on Rev. Moon and the Unification Church. He cited Acts 5 as his argument that Christians should refrain from attacking Moon's doctrines. In Acts 5:34-39, a Pharisee named Gamaliel advised the Jewish Council that if the action of Peter and John is of men it will be overthrown; but if it turns out to be of God, those who oppose it will find themselves fighting against God. Likewise, the minister said, we should heed Gamaliel's words and leave the Unification Church alone.

It is interesting that he did not mention the longevity and prosperity of the Mormons and the Jehovah Witnesses. Nevertheless, his remarks disturbed me deeply, for it was typical of the comments which I have frequently heard from Christians. That attitude, as well as the attitude that Moon and his teachings are so false that they must be a joke, have lulled the Christian church into passivity and have allowed Moon to go unchallenged. While a few Christian groups (primarily those who are labeled "Jesus Freaks" by the Unification Church, the mass media and even by some Christians) strongly opposed Moon's initial ingress into this country, the established Christian community was either ignorant of the insidious nature of his church or underestimated its spiritual significance.

Such is the judgment of the Lord upon the Christian church. Because of its own passivity it must struggle and suffer more anguish than if it had proclaimed the truth from the outset. As so often is the case, only after the mass media has exposed Moon have Christians in general begun to take issue with him.

The Unification Church, however, is not unique. There are numerous Christian counterfeits, old and new, plaguing our society. The Unification Church is just one symptom of a greater ill within the body of Christ. All the Christian counterfeits are signs of that disease: the lack of acceptance and love between the members of the body of Christ and complete submission to the head.

There are actually two species of "Christians" in the world. First are those who are Christians in name only, that is, those who in their minds justify their lives as being Christian, while cohabiting with the world. Their judgment is condemnation. Second are those genuine Christians who are wedded with Christ but who still do not know Jesus enough and love him enough and love each other enough to be able to present to the world a single picture of Christ. The judgment on these Christians is what it has been from the days of the Apostle John. In his first epistle John adjured Christians to "love one another, for love is from God" (1 John 4:7), and he admonished them not to listen to the Gnostics who were trying to pervert the gospel. As long as there are divisions within the Christian church and a lack of total fidelity to the Bridegroom, Satan will always conjure false pictures of Christ to confuse the world and disturb the body.

The Christian church has often sinned by being invisible. Either congregations are so averse to the world that they have hidden themselves and no one knows of their existence, not even the other members of the church, or they are so enamored with the world that there is hardly any distinction between the two. No wonder it has been easy for Satan to sneak in his own brand of church here and there, proclaim it as Christian and have the world believe it. The Christian church must not only contend with these false churches but with the lies about Christ as well.

But how can an individual Christian be responsible to know the doctrines of all the Christian counterfeits when there are so many? There is no need to be filled with all the knowledge of the world. To know Christ fully as Savior, Lord and God is sufficient. By that standard you will know who is of men and who is of God. If they are of men, it is our responsibility to shed light where there is darkness, for "you are the light of the world" (Matthew 5:14). If they are of God, "let us not love in word or speech but in deed and in truth" (1 John 3:18) those who are of God.

Moon and his followers do not confess that Jesus Christ is their Savior, Lord and God. So we must share the gospel with them and preach the truth in the Spirit of love. "In this the love of God was made manifest among us, that God has sent his only Son into the world, so that we might live through him" (1 John 4:9).

Grace/   The sincerity of the followers of Rev. Moon has awed many people, including Christians. Their devotion to the movement, their separation from the world and its evils, their love for each other and their joy have put numerous Christians to shame. To share the gospel with these people and not believe their sincerity is to speak in ignorance of the power of the Enemy; to share the gospel with them and be dumbfounded by their sincerity is to speak in ignorance of the power of the Lord. Their sincerity is authentic; otherwise they could not convince other people to surrender all. But their faith, their dedication, their love is based on works.

The telltale mark of many cults is that their system of salvation is established on works and not on grace. Paul warned the Christians at Colossae, "If with Christ you died to the elemental spirits of the universe, why do you live as if you still belonged to the world? Why do you submit to regulations, 'Do not handle, Do not taste, Do not touch.' . . . These have indeed an appearance of wisdom in promoting rigor of devotion and self-abasement and severity to the body" (Colossians 2:20-21, 23). The system through which the followers of Moon have to fulfill the Law of Indemnity does nothing less than displace the grace of God with the works of men.

All that has been said about the Unification Church in this book reflects a doctrine of works. Moon's teachings on perfection and salvation are systems through which an individual must attain perfection and salvation through works. The doctrine of Formation, Growth and Perfection is a blatant attempt by men to climb to heaven on a ladder of works. The Four Position Foundation is achieved through marriage, but marriage is only granted after fulfilling specific works. Fasting, fundraising and recruiting are all works under the Law of Indemnity.

God, however, has called us through his grace alone. Paul says, "For by grace you have been saved through faith; and this is not your own doing, it is the gift of God" (Ephesians 2:8). If we believe that our salvation depends on works, our eyes will be upon what we must do. If we believe that our salvation has been accomplished through God's loving grace, our eyes will be upon what God has done. Again Paul says, "If then you have been raised with Christ, seek the things that are above, where Christ is, seated at the right hand of God. Set your minds on things that are above, not on things that are on earth" (Colossians 3:1-2).

Clearly Moon has set his mind on earth. The defeat of communism, the establishment of his heavenly kingdom on earth, the indemnity of the individual, family, nation and world, the unification of science, politics and art with religion, his voracious appetite for real estate and his emphasis on "holy ground"—all manifest where his heart is set.

Moon has said that the relationship between himself and his followers is that of father and children, and that the relationship between Christ and his followers is that of master and servants. As a father Moon is a severe taskmaster who exacts much from his children. In reality, however, they are his slaves. Meanwhile, Christ, as our brother, has taken our hands and led us to our true Father. God is our Father . . . not Moon! "And because you are sons, God has sent the Spirit of his Son into our hearts, crying, 'Abba! Father!' So through God you are no longer a slave but a son, and if a son then an heir" (Galatians 4:6-7).

As children of God, our response to the followers of Moon and all others in the world is to share with them the way to God so that they too may be his children; and the way is Jesus who loved us and died for us.

"And with great power the apostles gave their testimony to the resurrection of the Lord Jesus, and great grace was upon them all" (Acts 4:33).

A BIBLICAL CRITIQUE

9

GOD'S TRUTH IS JESUS CHRIST. In him and by him all things were created and have their meaning. To know the truth is to know Jesus. To live in truth is to be in Jesus and to be with God.

The Word/   The Gospel of John, the epistles to the Colossians and Hebrews, and the first epistle of John are excellent biblical books to recommend to those people who have accepted Christ into their lives and have left the Unification Church and want a deeper understanding of Christ in contrast to Moon's teachings. Because these books emphasize the deity of Christ, the atonement and the discernment of false teachings pertaining to Christ, they are particularly helpful for sharing the gospel with those still in the movement. One of the primary aims of each of these works was to combat a growing heresy within the first-century church, and they are still effective in countering any heresy that would deny complete salvation in Christ.

There is, of course, one major obstacle to overcome if a biblical critique of the *Divine Principle* and the inner teachings of Rev.

Moon is to be effective. The adherents of the movement believe
that the Bible is not absolute truth. Moon himself is the final authority; the Bible is a textbook which only he has decoded. This
would seem to neutralize any critique of Moon based on Scripture.

Nevertheless, as Christians we must remember that there is a
power greater than Moon or the forces behind him. If the people with whom you are sharing the Lord Jesus are sincerely seeking the truth, the Spirit of Christ will restrain other influences
and plant within their hearts the desire to hear the gospel. If we
ourselves trust in the highest authority, we need not fear how to
prove the Bible is absolute. Certainly we should ourselves know
as much as we can about why the Bible is authoritative and accurate. And there are good books to help us.[1] But for our purpose
in witnessing to non-Christians, we can be confident that the
Word of God itself speaks with power to convict and convince. It
will prove itself as it has for centuries to those people who have
sought God.

The Apostle Paul predicted the sort of skepticism found in the
teachings of Moon. Consequently he made it clear to Timothy
that "all scripture is inspired by God" (2 Timothy 3:16). He further warned, "For the time is coming when people will not en-
dure sound teaching, but having itching ears they will accumu-
late for themselves teachers to suit their own likings, and will
turn away from listening to the truth and wander into myths"
(2 Timothy 4:3-4).

One of the most incredible myths is Moon's account of the
fall of Adam and Eve. The traditional account of Genesis 3 is
abandoned and replaced with an allegorical interpretation
which starts by declaring the tree of life to be the symbol of perfected Adam and the tree of knowledge to be the symbol of Eve.
It is here that Moon begins to introduce concepts which are alien
to the Bible.

As difficult as it is to understand how Satan could tempt Eve
with the fruit of herself, it takes an even greater leap of faith to
accept the logic of the following syllogism: It is the nature of man

to cover the area of transgression; Adam and Eve covered the sexual areas of their bodies; therefore they committed sexual sin and it is that sin which constitutes the fall.

Moon is clearly departing from the traditional understanding of the fall in favor of a doctrine which will neatly undermine the work of Christ and establish grounds for his own claim as the Messiah. By stating that the fall was sexual, Moon can thereby include the physical with the original sin of man. This sin, he further argues, was not completely expiated by Christ, because the nature of Christ's work was only spiritual. Thus, the Messiah must come again to redeem the physical part of sin. Moon, therefore, can use "the physical" as a basis for presenting any doctrinal principle which he wishes to make.

That it is the nature of man to cover the area of transgression is an extra-biblical principle which one needs to accept before the syllogism can proceed. Second, the notion that Eve had sexual contact with Satan has no biblical support whatsoever. Furthermore, there is no warrant in either the Old or New Testament for an interpretation of the fall along the spiritual and physical lines suggested in the *Divine Principle*. If people accept the *Divine Principle*'s interpretation of the fall, they do so because they place their faith in Rev. Moon himself and in the revelations which he claims to have received from God.

An obvious point of discord between the Bible and the *Divine Principle* is the idea that Cain is the fruit of Eve's relation with Satan. Genesis 4:1 flatly reads, "Now Adam knew Eve his wife, and she conceived and bore Cain." The *Divine Principle* does not merely read into the Scriptures additional material but flagrantly misrepresents what is clearly stated. If the followers of Moon truly believe in him, they must choose his word over the Bible.

A closer examination of Moon's interpretation of the fall also reveals another subtle hint of Satan's influence on his doctrine. It is questionable whether the *Divine Principle* leaves room for man's responsibility for the fall. If Eve was seduced by Satan and then in turn seduced Adam, were not both of them victims of Satan's nefarious desires rather than agents responsible for their

own actions, particularly since Eve did not know that her intended spouse was to be Adam until after she was seduced? That
would suggest that God did not make Adam and Eve capable of
withstanding temptation from Satan, which places the responsibility for sin squarely at the feet of God.

Traditionally, the fall has been understood by Christians to
consist of Adam and Eve's disobedience of a direct command of
God not to eat the fruit of the tree of the knowledge of good and
evil. Adam knew exactly what he was doing when he disobeyed.
"The Lord God commanded the man, saying, 'You may freely
eat from every tree of the garden; but of the tree of the knowledge of good and evil you shall not eat, for in the day that you
eat of it you shall die' " (Genesis 2:16-17). It was Adam's rebel-
lion, his direct disobedience, which constituted the fall.

Rev. Moon has said that after Christ first visited with him he
had to struggle with Satan for nine years. Finally he defeated
Satan and discovered the truth concerning the fall of man.
Moon's distortion of the Bible and the truth is actually no different from Adam and Eve's sin. Essentially what Adam and
Eve did was to disobey God's word and seek to be equal with
God. Moon also strayed from God's word in order to establish
the authority of his own words. No wonder Moon wants to alter
the true nature of the fall! It is too incriminating.

Moon's so-called spiritual struggle with Satan is in startling
contrast with Jesus in the wilderness. Each time Satan tempted
him, Jesus stood on the Word of God. Jesus did not seek to glorify himself or to discover truths (Hebrews 5:5). Jesus is the
truth.

Prophecy/   Throughout the Old and New Testaments there
are two series of prophecies foretelling the first and the second
comings of the Messiah. Psalm 22, Isaiah 53, Zechariah and
other works prophesy that the Messiah will come to suffer and
die for the sins of men. Daniel 7:13, Matthew 24:29-31, 1 Thessalonians 4:16-17 and other passages prophesy that the Messiah
will come to gather his people and reign as Lord.

Rev. Moon's misuse of Scriptures is no more blatant than when he interprets the Messianic prophecies. In Moon's teachings, it was not God's plan for Christ to die on the cross. The question then arises: If Christ had not died, how could the first series of prophecies have been fulfilled? Moon has two answers: First, God set before Israel two ways in which they could receive the Messiah. They could receive him as their king or they could crucify him. It was their choice, and they chose to crucify him. Second and more important, God foreknew how Israel would respond. Thus, God in his infinite wisdom knew that both prophecies would be fulfilled.

The problem with Moon's argument, however, is that the decision for which path Christ is to take would ultimately rest with the Jews not with Christ. Jesus, on the contrary, said, "Think not that I have come to abolish the law and the prophets; I have not come to abolish them but to fulfil them. For truly, I say to you, till heaven and earth pass away, not an iota, not a dot, will pass from the law until all is accomplished" (Matthew 5:17-18). He knew the course which he had to take. He also knew that he—not he with Moon or any other messiah—would fulfill all the prophecies. And, when he said to his Father, "Nevertheless not my will, but thine, be done" (Luke 22:42), he made the choice to die for us.

Moon also goes to great length to explain that the second coming will not be the Lord coming on the clouds as described in the second series of prophecies. He says that Christians are duplicating the same mistake the Jews committed when they rejected Jesus because he did not come as was prophesied by Daniel. Moon's argument is that the descriptions in the second series of prophecies are metaphoric and that the Lord of the Second Advent must be born of woman if he is to expiate man's physical sins. Of course, Moon has a personal stake in the doctrine. If the Lord is to come on the clouds, it would rule out Moon as the Messiah.

As to when the Messiah will come again, the *Divine Principle* may be correct in asserting that he will return in this present age.

The Bible indicates that God alone knows the time. Jesus said, "Of that day and hour no one knows, not even the angels of heaven, nor the Son, but the Father only" (Matthew 24:36). If Moon is right, therefore, it is only by accident.

As to the location of the origin of the Lord of the Second Advent, the *Divine Principle* ties together an incredible string of assertions. Again Moon misuses prophecy, this time from Revelation 7:2-4. First, his book asserts that "another angel" is the Messiah and not an actual angel. Second, it asserts that "the rising of the sun" is from the East and not from an eastward direction. Third, it asserts that the East refers to the Orient and not a more likely location such as the Middle East. Fourth, it asserts that the East refers to Korea, Japan and China and not any other oriental nation. Finally, it asserts that Korea is the birthplace of the Messiah. Why not claim Japan as the place referred to since she calls herself the land of "the rising sun"? To accept Korea as the birthplace is to rest the maximum of faith upon the minimum of logic.

Ironically, by expanding upon these verses from Revelation, Rev. Moon does fulfill one other verse from John's Revelation. Jesus warned in Revelation 22:18, "I warn every one who hears the words of the prophecy of this book: if anyone adds to them, God will add to him the plagues described in this book."

Just as the *Divine Principle* warns Christians against not heeding the revelations imparted to Moon, God has an appropriate warning to those who would follow Moon:

Then he said to me, "Son of man, have you seen what the elders of the house of Israel are doing in the dark, every man in his room of pictures? For they say, 'The Lord does not see us, the LORD has forsaken the land.' " He said also to me, "You will see still greater abominations which they commit."

Then he brought me to the entrance of the north gate of the house of the LORD; and behold, there sat women weeping for Tammuz. Then he said to me, "Have you seen this, O son of man? You will see still greater abominations than these."

And he brought me into the inner court of the house of the

LORD; and behold, at the door of the temple of the LORD, between the porch and the altar, were about twenty-five men, with their backs to the temple of the LORD, and their faces toward the east, worshiping the sun toward the east. Then he said to me, "Have you seen this, O son of man? Is it too slight a thing for the house of Judah to commit the abominations which they commit here, that they should fill the land with violence, and provoke me further to anger? Lo, they put the branch to their nose. Therefore I will deal in wrath; my eye will not spare, nor will I have pity; and though they cry in my ears with a loud voice, I will not hear them." (Ezekiel 8:12-18) Certainly this warning is not restricted to Moon and the Unification Church, nor do I wish to suggest, let alone prove, that Moon is the Antichrist. God is saying to Ezekiel, however, that there is an abomination greater than worshiping carved images or other gods. That is to pretend to be in the temple of the Lord and wait for another Savior and Lord. Judgment upon those who do this will be harsh indeed.

Paul warned the Christians against such teachings as the doctrines of Moon: "See to it that no man makes a prey of you by philosophy and empty deceit, according to human tradition, according to the elemental spirits of the universe, and not according to Christ" (Colossians 2:8).

Jesus Is Savior, Lord and God/   If Rev. Moon is to succeed in selling himself as the Lord of the Second Advent, he must severely discredit Jesus as the first Messiah. He cannot accomplish this by a total rejection of Jesus (as leaders of all Christian cults know). He must embrace Jesus, praise him and even witness in his name, but simultaneously he must teach that Jesus is neither the only Savior and Lord, nor is he God. It is essential for every Christian to know Jesus as Savior, Lord and God, not only to defend the faith but even more to walk in faith.

The *Divine Principle* argues that Jesus did not fulfill God's plan of total redemption. This was due to the Jews' failure to believe in Jesus because of John the Baptist. The Apostle John, however, said, "And many came to him; and they said, 'John did no sign, but everything that John said about this man was true.' And many believed in him there" (John 10:41-42).

Throughout his ministry John the Baptist pointed to Jesus as the Messiah, even directing some of the apostles to him. If anything, John opened the eyes of the Jews to the coming of the Messiah. Nevertheless, followers of the Unification Church argue that all the flattering references to John were made by those writers who had a limited understanding of the spiritual significance of John's actions. Yet, late in his ministry and long after John had been beheaded, Jesus himself said, "For John came to you in the way of righteousness" (Matthew 21:32).

Moon, however, contends that Jesus had to take the way of the cross, which was the lesser of two paths prophesied by the prophets. If the Jews had believed in him, Jesus would have taken the path leading to the establishment of the Kingdom of Heaven on earth. Jesus could then have redeemed people physically by marrying the perfect woman and have forgiven them spiritually by word of mouth.

By asserting that the work of Christ is incomplete, Moon can teach that man has need for a second messiah in order to be perfected. The writer to the Hebrews, however, says, "For by a single offering he [Christ] has perfected for all time those who are sanctified" (Hebrews 10:14). In other words, the washing away of sins he did "once for all when he offered up himself " (7:27). "Consequently he is able for all time to save those who draw near to God through him, since he always lives to make intercession for them" (7:25).

If the work of Christ is complete, therefore, another messiah is unnecessary. In fact, Luke makes it explicit: "And there is salvation in no one else, for there is no other name under heaven given among men by which we must be saved" (Acts 4:12). Paul agrees, "For there is one God, and there is one mediator between God and men, the man Christ Jesus, who gave himself as a ransom for all, the testimony to which was borne at the proper time" (1 Timothy 2:5-6).

Since Christ has atoned for our sins, he has not merely atoned some of our sins, "but if we walk in the light as he is in the light, we have fellowship with one another, and the blood of Jesus his Son cleanses us from all sin" (1 John 1:7). Furthermore, "since therefore the children share in flesh and blood, he himself likewise partook of the same nature, that through death he might destroy him who has the power of death, that is, the devil" (Hebrews 2:14).

The first time Jesus came to the world, he came to save the lost from sin: "And we have seen and testify that the Father has sent his Son to be the Savior of the world" (1 John 4:14). When Christ returns, he returns not to atone for sin: "Christ, having been offered once to bear the sins of many, will appear a second time, not to deal with sin, but to save those who are eagerly waiting for him" (Hebrews 9:28).

Jesus came and redeemed those who believe in him. He has washed away all their sins and made them perfect and holy before God. He is the only mediator, for he died once for all. He has defeated sin, death and Satan, and when he returns, he returns to take us home to heaven. Jesus is *the* Savior.

But Jesus is also Lord. Throughout the New Testament he is called "Lord," and those who have faith in him do likewise. Nevertheless, many people have been called "Lord" or "Master." Moon is one. So what distinguishes Jesus from the others? Interestingly the prophetic book of Isaiah and the Gospel of John both present the concept of "I AM." How they relate to each other may indicate why only Jesus is Lord.

From Chapter 41 to 46 of Isaiah, God frequently says, "I am . . .": "I am God" (Isaiah 43:13; 45:22; 46:9); "I am the first and I am the last" (44:6; cf. 41:4); "I am the Lord, who made all things" (44:24; cf. 45:7-8, 12); "I am he who blots out your transgressions" (43:25); "I am the Lord" (43:11, 15; 44:24; 45:6-7, 18; cf. 41:4, 13).

Likewise, throughout the Gospel of John, Jesus says, "I am . . .": "I am the bread of life" (John 6:35); "I am the light of the world" (8:12); "Before Abraham was, I am" (8:58); "I am the door" (10:9); "I am the good shepherd" (10:11); "I am the resurrection, and the life" (11:25); "I am the way, and the truth, and the life" (14:6); and "I am he" (8:24).

Although the "I am's" of Jesus are metaphorical, while the "I am's" of God are forthright, the "I am's" of both books are essentially the same. Texts from each say that he has always been, that within him is the sustenance for life, that through him is salvation.[2] Most importantly each demands that man's total vision be focused on him. If the parallel descriptions are not enough to tie together God the Father and Jesus the Son, another statement of Jesus does: "I and the Father are one" (John 10:30).

Since Jesus declares this oneness, and since the Father says, "I am the LORD, and there is no other" (Isaiah 45:6), it follows that there must be no denigration of Jesus' status as Lord. The Bible and Moon part company, therefore, when Moon asserts that he has a role to play as Master and Savior.

If Jesus is Lord, there is no place for Moon. Jesus demands our all if he is to be Lord over our lives: "If any man would come after me, let him deny himself and take up his cross daily and follow me. For whoever would save his life will lose it; and whoever loses his life for my sake, he will save it" (Luke 9:23-24).

For Jesus to be our Lord, we must surrender ourselves completely to him, not merely our time, our money and our allegiance, but our all. Then, we can say, like Paul, "For although there may be so-called gods in heaven or on earth—as indeed there are many "gods" and many "lords"—yet for us there is one God, the Father, from whom are all things and for whom we exist, and one Lord, Jesus Christ, through whom are all things and through whom we exist" (1 Corinthians 8:5-6).

That all things exist through Jesus is a mark of his deity. In fact, biblical writers state that the world was created through Jesus (John 1:3, 10; Hebrews 1:2; Colossians 1:16). It is true that Jesus never said, "I am God." Consequently Moon does not hesitate to twist into his own line of reasoning the verses substantiating Jesus' divinity. Such verses as "I am in my Father" (John 14:20) are juxtaposed with such verses as "My God, my God, why hast thou forsaken me?" (Matthew 27:46) to prove that Jesus is not God; for how could he forsake himself? Certainly there is a distinction between Jesus and the Father, but it does not follow that he does not possess the full deity of God. Rather, Paul said to the Colossians, "In him [Christ] the whole fulness of deity dwells bodily, and you have come to fulness of life in him, who is the head of all rule and authority" (Colossians 2:9-10).

Paul also stated that Jesus "was in the form of God" (Philippians 2:6). John illuminated Christ's divinity even further: "In the beginning was the Word, and the Word was with God, and the Word was God. . . . And the Word became flesh and dwelt among us, full of grace and truth; we have beheld his glory, glory as of the only Son from the Father" (John 1:1,14).

Jesus himself said at the last supper, "And now, Father, glorify thou me in thy own presence with the glory which I had with thee before the world was made" (John 17:5). Here Jesus claims that he was not a part of creation but with the Father from the beginning. "Father," he continued, "I desire that they also whom thou hast given me, may be with me where I am, to behold my glory which thou hast given me in thy love for me before the foundation of the world" (17:24). The Father's love for Jesus not only confirms his existence before the foundation of the world, but also shows that God is a personal God and that the relationship between God the Father and God the Son is a personal relationship.

To say that Jesus is God is not to divorce him from his humanity, however. This is what the Gnostics did in the first century and what the cults have done ever since. This is what Moon is doing now. Although few would say that Jesus is God, most separate Jesus' spiritual life from his physical life. The most glaring example is Moon's doctrine on the physical resurrection of Christ.

Moon employs two passages to support his claim that Jesus "was a being transcendent of time and space" (DP 360). One incident occurs when "the doors were shut, but Jesus came and stood among them" (John 20:26). Moon reasons that Jesus could not

have been physical if the doors were shut. The next verse, however, counts against that deduction: "Then he said to Thomas,
'Put your finger here, and see my hands; and put out your hand,
and place it in my side; do not be faithless, but believing.' "

The second incident occurs when Jesus walked with his disciples who did not recognize him. The crucial verse is Luke 24:
31: "And their eyes were opened and they recognized him; and
he vanished out of their sight." The language can be read in favor of Moon or as a colorful description of the incident. The following verses, however, settle any dispute over Christ's physical
resurrection:

As they were saying this, Jesus Himself stood among them.
But they were startled and frightened, and supposed that they
saw a spirit. And he said to them, "Why are you troubled, and
why do questionings rise in your hearts? See my hands and my
feet, that it is I myself; handle me, and see; for a spirit has not
flesh and bones as you see that I have." And while they still
disbelieved for joy, and wondered, he said to them, "Have you
anything here to eat?" They gave him a piece of a broiled fish,
and he took it and ate it before them. (Luke 24:36-43)

Jesus Christ is our Savior, because he died for all our sins and
because he has conquered death and Satan. He is our Lord and
Master, because he guides us with love and truth to his Father,
and because he cares for us like a shepherd. He is our God, because he is the only begotten Son of God the Father and because
through him we were created.

Judgment on the World/   Many people have died from illnesses because their effort was to cure the symptom rather than
the disease. It may be fatal to believe that all will be well once a
symptom is treated and eliminated. The Lord in his wisdom created pain, signs and other manifestations to indicate when something is wrong with us. This is likewise true with the spiritual
condition of the world.

Throughout time, society has been confronted with symptoms of its spiritual illness. Today one of the symptoms is the

presence of Sun Myung Moon and the Unification Church. Several groups of parents and other organizations who busily engage in trying to eliminate Moon's movement are merely taking aspirins for the headache-symptoms of an oncoming stroke. Even if they should succeed in banishing Moon from the face of the earth, another false messiah could soon rise up to take his place. For the basic problem will still not have been treated.

It is a mistake to believe that the world can cure the world; the world itself is corrupt. "They know not, neither will they understand; they walk on in darkness: all the foundations of the earth are out of course" (Ps. 82:5, AV). When Adam fell, sin entered the world and has ailed men ever since; sin is the true illness. But we should not repeat the mistake of believing that the symptoms are the disease. Sins, such as murder, injustice, immorality, sorcery, are only the manifestations of sin; sin is separation from God. Our independence and alienation from God is the true cause of our illness.

Praise God! He has sent us a physician; he has offered a cure. Jesus Christ his Son is a panacea for all illnesses, but particularly for our separation from God. "For in him all the fulness of God was pleased to dwell, and through him to reconcile to himself all things, whether in earth or in heaven, making peace by the blood of his cross" (Colossians 1:19-20).

The world, however, will not receive the physician Jesus Christ, because the price is too great. It costs everything to be cured; and so, the world tries to find a cheaper remedy. And this is the judgment on the world, that there is no other remedy. "For God sent the Son into the world, not to condemn the world, but that the world might be saved through him. He who believes in him is not condemned; he who does not believe is condemned already, because he has not believed in the name of the only Son of God" (John 3:17-18).

The illness in man is sin. The cause of sin is separation from God. A symptom of the separation of the world from God is presence of Moon and his movement. The pain of man's separation from God is the loss of their children. The judgment upon those who have sinned is death. The physician is Jesus Christ. The cost of being cured by Christ is total surrender to him. The cure is everlasting life with him.

Faith/   To have faith in Jesus Christ, to believe in the truth, is to look at the Lord, confess to him our sin, repent and trust him with our lives. Though it is a source of great power, faith is unassuming. Though it is the strength of an individual, faith is not self-regarding. Like the eye, faith looks at the object and not upon itself. Possessing faith is "looking to Jesus the pioneer and perfecter of our faith" (Hebrews 12:2).

Many people are discouraged because they wonder if they have faith or not. They feel that they must have the assurance of their belief; they think that they must have the conviction of their belief; and that if they lack these qualities, then they must lack faith. But the assurance of things hoped for and the conviction of things not seen are not ways of appropriating faith; they are the fruit of faith. Like the fruit of the Spirit, they may not always be evident, but that does not mean that the Spirit is not indwelling.

Faith is not our ability to believe or our capacity to hope. Faith is a gift of God. Faith depends on us only insofar as we accept this gift and gaze upon the giver. Faith is looking at the Lord instead of ourselves or the world. Faith is looking at the Lord because we love him and need him. The goal of indemnity in Moon's theology may be perfection, "but the aim of our charge is love that issues from a pure heart and a good conscience and sincere faith" (1 Timothy 1:5).

During the early years of Jacob's walk with the Lord, whenever the Lord wanted to speak with Jacob, he spoke to him in a dream. Jacob was too cunning and self-willed to be able to see the Lord face to face. But after the struggle at Peniel when Jacob was finally molded into a humble servant, the Lord was able to communicate with Jacob face to face just as he did with his fathers before him.

After Miriam and Aaron spoke against Moses in the wilderness, the Lord responded, "If there is a prophet among you, I the LORD make myself known to him in a vision, I speak with him in a dream. Not so with my servant Moses; he is entrusted with all my house. With him I speak mouth to mouth, clearly, and not in dark speech; and he beholds the form of the LORD" (Numbers 12: 6-8).

Moon encourages his followers to have dreams and visions of himself, but God wants us to speak with him person to person. It may be difficult at first to look at the Lord, and even more difficult to see him. But if our love for him grows, our looking will become natural and our seeing will be constant.

A SPIRITUAL DISCERNMENT

10

LIFE IN THE SPIRIT IS EVERLASTING. It is abundant and free. It is full of joy and peace. Because this life is founded in Jesus, it is not aimless but empowered with meaning. It is not bound by death, for Jesus has conquered death. The Spirit of Jesus dwells in us that we may have this life and live as Jesus lived.

Winning through Intimidation/ Today, however, there is another power which is gradually casting its shadow across the land. It brings not life but death, not love but fear. These past years the Evil One has been exerting his influence in every segment of our society—religion, government, literature, music, entertainment, science, business, even the Christian church itself. His aim is to erect a super-spiritual structure through which he can rule the world.

Whether the Evil One will succeed in achieving his desires and thereby fulfill the prophecies of the last days is not known to any man. Nevertheless, ours is a time of great spiritual struggle; though few see it now, all of us will come to know it. Ours is a time when battle lines are being drawn, and those who are for the Lord must now declare it; for only the people of God have the power to oppose the forces of evil.

Eastern mysticism, Western rationalism, communism, materialism, immorality are but a few of Satan's tools; and as each nail is hammered into its place by these tools, the day comes nearer when all the land will be in the shadow of his structure. Satan's only fear is the power of the Lord, which is greater and has already defeated him.

In a minor skirmish a decade ago, for example, Satan was routed. The front cover of *Time* magazine (April 8, 1966) proclaimed that God was dead. This was a great victory for the Enemy. Here was the fruit of all the doubts which he had planted in men's minds for the past centuries in the West. Now he was ready to feed their hungry souls with the beliefs of the East, which he had also been developing for centuries. But then, at the end of the sixties and the beginning of the seventies, Satan was thwarted. The Lord had been preparing his people for this challenge. And when the time was right, he sent them—young and old, people of all races both within the establishment and within the counterculture—out to witness on the streets and on the beaches, at colleges and at airports. Everyone was being confronted with a living Jesus, and this witness was winning many victories.

Any goals which Satan has achieved have come by tremendous struggle and at costly delay. The Enemy has suffered a setback. In counterattack he has been setting up Christian counterfeits, such as the Children of God, The Way and particularly the Unification Church. With so many different kinds of people opposing Rev. Moon and his movement, many Christians wonder how Moon could possibly play a role in Satan's plan. But this opposition to Moon has had side effects on true Christian witness. By presenting a pseudo-Christian such as Moon to the world, Satan has succeeded in again turning off the world to genuine Christianity and its people. Worse, Satan has crippled Christian witnessing. People are not only turned off to the witnessing which is done by Moon's followers, but by Christ's followers as well.

Sharing the gospel of Christ, however, is not ultimately damaged by how the world reacts but by how Christians are intimidated. In the late sixties and early seventies it was easy to share Jesus with a stranger. Generally they were friendly and open. Today, however, people are cold and withdrawn and sometimes hostile. It takes power and courage and love in large amounts to share Jesus, and because too few of us have these qualities we have been intimidated by the Enemy.

Oh, we can say that the Lord is not leading us or that we are spiritually too mature for that sort of work. We can reason that God is in control and that he will take care of the lost. But most of the time these are just excuses to mask our fears. The devastating weapon of the Enemy has always been intimidation, and he is succeeding in muting the voice of the church.

If we believe in Christ, if we believe there is the Enemy, if we believe that the Enemy is constructing his kingdom, if we believe we have the truth which has defeated him and will deliver those who are lost, isn't it time for us to stand up and say so—not to our intimate Christian friends, nor in the closets of our churches, but to people in the world? If we love Christ and those who do not have Christ, where is our voice? Where is the life of Jesus living in us?

It does not matter whether Satan seems to succeed or not, because his victory can only be hollow. Ultimately he will be cast into the pit. What matters is whether we love Jesus enough not to be intimidated by the Enemy.

"And now, Lord, look upon their threats, and grant to thy servants to speak thy word with all boldness, while thou stretchest out thy hand to heal, and signs and wonders are performed through the name of thy holy servant Jesus" (Acts 4:29-30).

The Puppet Master/   I have been frequently asked: Do you believe that Rev. Moon is deceiving his followers for material wealth and political power or does Moon actually believe that he is the Messiah? Apparently both are true.

Moon is probably trying to deceive everyone outside his inner circle. I have talked with many former members who say they were told one thing, only to learn later that what they were told wasn't true. In fact, if the bulk of his followers were in on the workings of Moon's financial plans and political aspirations, would they continue to sacrifice their lives in solicitation of funds and in seemingly endless lectures on theology?

His messianic leanings were probably developed early in his life. Unquestionably he was a spiritually sensitive young man. This type of person, however, can be sensitive to spiritual forces from either side, depending upon other character traits. No doubt Moon had a spiritual experience when he was sixteen, but was it Jesus who confronted him? Certainly the Jesus of the New Testament did not commission him to complete his unfinished task. Perhaps Moon was approached by Satan or one of his associates pretending to be Christ and who appealed to Moon's natural and human desire for glory or power.

It is likewise probable that Moon engaged in a spiritual struggle the following nine years. Again, however, I suggest that he was thoroughly deceived in what occurred and what resulted. He did not discover the truth of the fall of man, but was given a lie to spread. He did not defeat Satan, but was himself won over.

Could it be that Satan cleverly manipulated Moon's weaknesses to persuade Moon to believe that they were the sins of other men? Was Satan securely tying these weaknesses to himself to become powerful strings between him and Moon? "Let no one disqualify you, insisting on self-abasement and worship of angels, taking his stand on visions he has seen, puffed up without reason by his sensuous mind" (Colossians 2:18).

Two of Moon's weaknesses stand out most clearly. The first is his preoccupation with sexuality. Moon has been beset with controversies concerning his sexual behavior during the early years of his church and the number of times he has been married; he is also bent on fathering twelve children by his present wife to match the twelve tribes of Israel. In his church, fornication is considered the worst sin and marriage is essential for complete salvation. In his teachings, man's original sin is sexual; Jesus failed to marry and produce offspring; and the Lord of the Second Advent must marry the perfect mate. These are but a few examples of the presence of sexuality in every facet of Moon's life and thought.

His second outstanding weakness is pride. When Moon says that he has suffered, he does not say that God comforted him but that he has comforted God. When Moon says that there is a victory, he does not give the glory to God but to himself. When he speaks of truth or love or any other virtue, he inevitably refers to himself. Furthermore, everything Christ has done or accomplished, Moon says that he has surpassed. All the glory in the world would not be sufficient for Moon, but Jesus said, "He who speaks on his own authority seeks his own glory; but he who seeks the glory of him who sent him is true, and in him there is no falsehood" (John 7:18).

If Satan has used sexuality and pride to manipulate Moon, he has done likewise to those around Moon, though in a far less self-satisfying way. For them sexual conduct has become an oppressive law under which to live. Meanwhile they must constantly pay homage to the pride of their master. Peter said, "But false prophets also arose among the people, just as there will be false teachers among you, who will secretly bring in destructive heresies, even denying the Master who bought them, bringing upon themselves swift destruction. And many will follow their licentiousness, and because of them the way of truth will be reviled. And in their greed they will exploit you with false words" (2 Peter 2:1-3).

Moon may have a strong hold on his followers, but the strings do not begin with him. Moon himself is more deceived than those whom he deceives. Moon is not the puppet master. Moon is the master puppet. Satan is the puppet master.

Judgment on Satan and His Host/   The power of Rev. Moon

has crushed many people's hopes of ever defeating him either in the courts or through agencies of the government. Moon possesses tremendous wealth; exercises political influence; and worse, has spiritual support. Even should he be stripped of his followers and his political ties, he still has the finances and real estate to do much of the bidding of his master. Should Moon himself be reduced in authority and power, Satan would merely replace him with another vassal.

A viewpoint such as this, however, is secondary compared to the overall struggle between the Lord Jesus and the Enemy. There is not only joy in the fact that Christ has already defeated Satan, but secure hope in the ultimate ruination of Satan and his hosts.

And then the lawless one will be revealed, and the Lord Jesus will slay him with the breath of his mouth and destroy him by his appearing and his coming. The coming of the lawless one by the activity of Satan will be with all power and with pretended signs and wonders, and with all the wicked deception for those who are to perish, because they refused to love the truth and so be saved. Therefore God sends upon them a strong delusion to make them believe what is false, so that all may be condemned who did not believe the truth but had pleasure in unrighteousness. (2 Thessalonians 2:8-12)

There are many reasons for the Lord's judgment of Rev. Moon and his followers—too many in fact to list. Three should suffice: First is Moon's teaching about spirits and his experiences with them. To exhort his followers to seek the aid of human spirits and not the Holy Spirit approaches outright defiance of God. His communications with Arthur Ford's Fletcher and other spirits echo Saul's iniquity: "So Saul died for his unfaithfulness; he was unfaithful to the LORD in that he did not keep the command of the LORD, and also consulted a medium, seeking guidance, and did not seek guidance from the Lord. Therefore the LORD slew him" (1 Chronicles 10:13-14).

Second, in 1960, Moon married Hak Ja Han and proclaimed it "the Marriage of the Lamb" in reference to the Apostle John's visions. "Let us rejoice and exult and give him the glory, for the marriage of the Lamb has come, and his Bride has made herself ready" (Revelation 19:7). In this verse John foresees the beautiful marriage between the Lord Jesus and his church. Moon in his vanity, however, claims the wedding for himself, and thus he commits a despicable sacrilege equaled by few.

Third, and most blasphemous of all, Moon declares that Jesus failed to save men because he died on the cross! Then Moon adds that he himself will fulfill that which Christ left undone! It is as if Moon was the one who jeered and challenged Jesus: "Let the Christ, the King of Israel, come down now from the cross, that we may see and believe" (Mark 15:32). The bodyguards of Moon may protect him from God's love, but what will they do against God's wrath?

As for Satan, his end is certain: "And the devil who had deceived them was thrown into the lake of fire and sulphur where the beast and the false prophet were, and they will be tormented day and night forever and ever" (Revelation 20:10).

The Enemy and his host may wield a stronger power than men's; the swords of the Enemy may have been forged in the fires of hell; but they have no power over the Lord's own.

But through Christ!   But through the Lord Jesus Christ there is everlasting joy and peace. Christians can still hope and, yes, pray that Rev. Moon will change his mind, repent, give up his false teaching about God, himself and mankind's plight. So long as Moon lives there is yet time for him to seek after God and find him. For Rev. Moon, as for all people true salvation is as close as this: believing in Christ and confessing him openly as Lord and Savior.

The word is near you, on your lips and in your heart (that is, the word of faith which we preach); because, if you confess with your lips that Jesus is Lord and believe in your heart that God raised him from the dead, you will be saved. For man believes with his heart and so is justified, and he confesses with his lips and so is saved. (Romans 10:8-10)

NOTES

Chapter 1

[1]"Sun Myung Moon, a Biography," a leaflet published by the Unification Church in Berkeley, California, p. 1.

[2]Ibid., p. 2.

[3]"The Candlelit World of Pastor Moon," *Crusade*, September 1974, p. 21.

[4]"The Church's Birth in Pusan," taken from a talk 28 August 1974 by Kwang Yol Yoo. *New Hope News*, Washington, D. C., 23 December 1974, p. 24.

[5]Hedley Donovan (editor), "Up Front," *People*, 20 October 1975, p. 8.

[6]Jane Day Mook, "The Unification Church," *A. D.*, May 1974, p. 34.

[7]"God's Hope for America," a sermon by Sun Myung Moon, 21 October 1973, from the book *Day of Hope*, published by the Unification Church (no copyright and no date), p. 72.

[8]"Rev. Moon mobilizing to bring God to U.S.A.," *The Daily News*, Tarrytown, New York, 3 October 1973.

[9]"Introduction" to *Day of Hope*, p. vii.

[10]"The New Messiah and the Founder of God in History," a sermon by Moon, March 1972. *Day of Hope*, p. 15.

[11]"On Leadership," a sermon by Moon, 9 November 1973. *Day of Hope*, p. 328.

[12]"Evangelist talks on Watergate," *Arkansas Democrat*, 22 March 1974.

[13]For an extensive analysis of Moon's financial holdings, see Chris Welles, "The Eclipse of Sun Myung Moon," *New York*, 27 September 1976, pp. 32-38.

Chapter 2

[1]Quotations from the *Divine Principle* are derived from the 1973 English edition, a translation from the original Korean. This second edition is different from the first English edition (1966) in a number of areas. Members of the Unification Church contend that the second edition is a text improved in translation, while others cite gross errors of interpretation of prophecy and Scriptures which could not withstand scriptural criticism in the first edition.

[2]Sun Myung Moon, "God's Hope for America," *Christianity in Crisis* (Washington, D. C.: HSA-UWC, Inc. [Holy Spirit Association-Unification World Christianity] 1974), p. 60.

[3]Ibid., p. 60.

[4]Sun Myung Moon, a sermon at the Portland Director's Conference, 14 April 1974, from *Day of Hope*, p. 410.

[5]Sun Myung Moon, "God's Hope for America," p. 67.

[6]Sun Myung Moon, "America in God's Providence," *New Hope* (Washington, D. C.: HSA-UWC, Inc., 1973), p. 16.

[7]*Analysis of the Present Day* (Washington, D. C.: HSA-UWC, Inc. 1973), p. 16.

[8]John D. Marks, "Shadows on Rev. Moon's Beams," *Chicago Tribune*, 10 November 1974, Section 2, p. 1.

9"Rev. Moon's Cosmic Truths," *San Francisco Chronicle*, 19 January 1974.

10Jerry Carroll, "Moon's Plan to Stop Communism," *San Francisco Chronicle*, 10 December 1975.

11Richard H. Ichord's written reply to Mr. Denzel Clark of Ft. Leavenworth, Kansas.

12John Cotter, "Rev. Moon seeks power through 'gospel,' " *Chicago Tribune*, 14 December 1975, p. 12.

13Jack Anderson, "The Speaker and a Moonie," *Long Island Press*, 9 December 1975, p. 19.

14"Mad about Moon," *Time* magazine, 10 November 1975, p. 44; and "Significance of the Training Session," *Master Speaks*, 17 May 1973, pp. 5, 7.

15John Cotter, p. 1; and "Parents' Day," *Master Speaks*, 24 March 1974, p. 9.

16Chuck Alexander, "Federal Probe of 'Moonie' Activities Sought," *The Wichita Eagle*, 13 January 1976, p. 1.

Chapter 3

1"One Big, Happy Family," *Newsweek*, 15 October 1973, p. 54.

2William J. Petersen, *Those Curious New Cults* (New Canaan, Conn.: Keats Publishing, 1975), pp. 247-48.

3Sun Myung Moon, "The New Messiah and the Formula of God in History," March 1972, sermon from *Day of Hope*, p. 15.

4*The Rising Tide*, 14 January 1974.

Chapter 4

1William Moore, "Rev. Moon's Cosmic Truths," *San Francisco Chronicle*, 19 January 1974.

2Ken Sudo, "Christology," from the *120-Day Training Manual* used at the International Unification Church Training Center in Barrytown, New York (no copyright or date), p. 328.

3Ibid., p. 236.

4Ibid., "Sin and Salvation," pp. 41-42.

5*Christian Crusade Weekly*, Tulsa, Oklahoma, 9 December 1973; and *Day of Hope*, p. 135.

6Berkeley Rice, "Honor Thy Father Moon," *Psychology Today*, January 1976, pp. 42, 45.

7Ken Sudo, "The Fall of Man," from the *120-Day Training Manual*, p. 198.

8Ibid., "Foundation for the Messiah," p. 61.

9Ibid., "Midway Position," p. 58.

10Ibid., "World Affairs," p. 110.

11John Cotter, "Don't Underestimate the 'Moon' Children," *The News-Sun*, Waukegan, Illinois, 23 December 1975, p. 6B.

12Margaret Bowers, "Sun Myung Moon Has Taken Our Daughter," *Eternity*, April 1976, pp. 30, 59; and "Significance of the Training Session," *Master Speaks*, 17 May 1973, p. 12.

13Sun Myung Moon, Portland Director's Conference, 14 April 1974, *Day of Hope*, p. 411.

Chapter 5

[1] Sun Myung Moon, "I believe in you," a sermon at the National Director's Conference, Washington, D. C., 31 January 1974, *New Hope*, p. 228.
[2] Ken Sudo, "Attendance," *120-Day Training Manual*, p. 151.
[3] John Cotter, "Peril Security of Moon Crusade," *Chicago Tribune*, 18 December 1975, section 3, p. 18.
[4] Ken Sudo, "Attendance," p. 152.
[5] Ibid., "Family Problems," p. 160.
[6] Ibid., "The Fall of Man," p. 203.
[7] Sara Perron, her testimony from "Practical Aspects of Training," *120-Day Training Manual*, p. 345.
[8] Ken Sudo, "How to be a Good Leader," *120-Day Training Manual*, p. 400.
[9] Ibid., "Foundation of Faith," p. 73.
[10] Ibid., "Attendance," p. 153.
[11] Ibid., "Foundation of Faith," p. 72.
[12] Ibid., "Practical Aspects of Training," p. 389.

Chapter 6

[1] Judy Shuler, *Anchorage Daily Times*, 17 April 1974, *New Hope*, p. 386.
[2] Ken Sudo, "The Meaning of Brothers and Sisters," from the *120-Day Training Manual*, p. 166.
[3] Young Oon Kim, *Divine Principle and Its Application*, (Washington, D. C.: HSA-UWC, 1968), p. 76.
[4] Ibid., p. 78.
[5] Ibid., p. 93.

Chapter 7

[1] Sun Myung Moon, "Significance of the Training Session," translated by Won Pok Choi, from *Master Speaks*, 17 May 1973, p. 5. (Each lecture's pages are renumbered within the *Master Speaks*.)
[2] Sun Myung Moon, "Victory or Defeat," translated by Won Pok Choi, from *Master Speaks*, 31 March 1973, p. 1.
[3] Sun Myung Moon, "Parent's Day Address," translated by Won Pok Choi, from *Master Speaks*, 3 April 1973, p. 2.
[4] Sun Myung Moon, "Christmas in Heart," translated by Bo Hi Pak, from *Master Speaks*, 25 December 1973, p. 4.
[5] Ibid., p. 6.
[6] Sun Myung Moon, "Parent's Day Address," p. 3.
[7] Sun Myung Moon, "The Way," translated by Won Pok Choi, from *Master Speaks*, 30 June 1974, p. 4.
[8] Sun Myung Moon, "Our Shame," translated by Won Pok Choi, from *Master Speaks*, 11 March 1973, p. 3.
[9] Sun Myung Moon, "Opening Talk—Morning Session," translated by David S. C. Kim, from *Master Speaks*, 4 July 1973, p. 3.
[10] Ken Sudo, "Family Problems," from the *120-Day Training Manual*, p. 160.

[11] Ibid., p. 222.

[12] Ibid., p. 362.

[13] Sun Myung Moon, "Portland Director's Conference," translated by Bo Hi Pak, from *Master Speaks*, 14 April 1974, p. 8.

[14] Sun Myung Moon, "Important Person," translated by Won Pok Choi, from *Master Speaks*, 10 June 1973, p. 6.

[15] Sun Myung Moon, "Parent's Day Address," p. 3.

[16] Sun Myung Moon, "Jacob's Course and Our Life in Faith," from *Master Speaks*, 27 May 1973, p. 13.

[17] Sun Myung Moon, "The Path of Abel," translated by Won Pok Choi, from *Master Speaks*, 4 March 1973, p. 10.

[18] Ibid.

[19] Young Oon Kim, *Divine Principle and Its Application*, p. 49.

[20] Sun Myung Moon, "Jacob's Course and Our Life in Faith," p. 10.

[21] Kwang-Yol Yoo, "Unification Church history from the early days," *New Hope News*, 7 October 1974, p. 7.

[22] Young Oon Kim, p. 1.

[23] Ibid., p. 97.

[24] Sun Myung Moon, "The Restoration of Heart," translated by Won Pok Choi, from *Master Speaks*, 20 February 1973, p. 7.

[25] Arthur Ford, *Unknown But Known* (New York: Signet Mystic, 1968), p. 120.

[26] "Moon Landing in Manhattan," *Time* magazine, 30 September 1974, p. 68.

[27] Arthur Ford, p. 136.

[28] Sun Myung Moon, "The Day of Victory Over Resentment," translated by Won Pok Choi, from *Master Speaks*, 1 May 1974, p. 9.

[29] Sun Myung Moon, "The Path We Tread," translated by Won Pok Choi, from *Master Speaks*, 25 August 1974, p. 10.

Chapter 8

[1] See, for example, the comments of E. Mansell Pattison of the department of psychiatry and human behavior, University of California, Irvine, in *Eternity*, April 1976, p. 29.

[2] Jack Buckley, "The Doubtful Ethics of Deprogramming," *Eternity*, April 1976, p. 30.

Chapter 9

[1] See, for example, the brief but excellent booklet by John Stott, *The Authority of the Bible* (Downers Grove, IL: InterVarsity Press, 1974). For an extensive treatment see Gordon Wenham, *Christ and the Bible* (Downers Grove, Ill.: InterVarsity Press, 1972).

[2] Also refer to Revelation 21:6.